Pennsylvania Dutch Country

W9-BGZ-811

By Margaret Gates, Susan Jurgelski and John Gattuso

"Who Are The Amish?" by Donald Kraybill

Additional reviews by Judith Rollman, Mary Alice Bitts, Mimi Brodeur, Peggy Schmidt and Rochelle Shenk

◆

Photographs by Keith Baum

Stone Creek Publications
Milford, New Jersey

Stone Creek Publications
460 Shire Road
Milford, NJ 08848
stocreek@aol.com

Library of Congress Catalog Card
Number: 98-60031

ISBN 0-9656338-1-0

Every effort has been made to
provide readers with accurate information. However, prices and other
items change often. Call ahead to
verify information. The writers and
publisher cannot accept responsi-
bility for the experience of readers
while traveling. Maps are not to scale.

Please forward all comments, sug-
gestions and corrections to Getaway
Guides, Stone Creek Publications,
460 Shire Road, Milford, NJ 08848,
Attn: Pennsylvania Dutch Country.
Or send e-mail to stocreek@aol.com.

Cover Photograph by Jerry Irwin

Design by Mary Kay Garttmeier

Special thanks to Edward A. Jardim
for editorial assistance.

*To Annette Jurgelski, Edith Campbell
and Jennifer Downey – S.J.*

To John, Drew and Joseph – M.G.

Manufactured in the United States
of America.

Table of Contents

Introduction & History

The first thing you should know about Pennsylvania Dutch Country is that the people who settled here two centuries ago weren't Dutch at all. They were "Deutsch" – German. There were others, of course. English, French, Scottish. But the folks who put the most indelible stamp on the place were immigrants from Germany and Switzerland.

What brought them here? Good advertising, for one thing. William Penn spread the word in the Old Country about the haven he had established across the ocean, and settlers from all over Europe responded. Among them were a group of religious dissenters known as Mennonites and a related sect, the Amish. Persecuted in Europe, they settled first near Philadelphia in 1683 and later pushed into the hinterlands around Lancaster County. Followers of other sects came, too, including Moravians, Lutherans and Brethren, all of whom are still active in the area. The best-known are the Amish, particularly the Old Order Amish, whose placid 19th-century way of life has come to characterize the "plain folk" of the area.

An Amish boy takes a break from farm work. Above, Mennonites take their name from Menno Simons, a Dutch priest who broke with the Church in 1536.

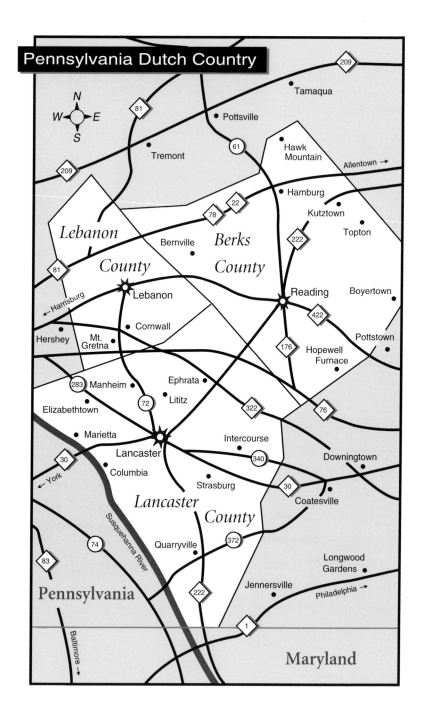

Pennsylvania Dutch Country

Tamaqua

Pottsville

Tremont

Hawk Mountain

Allentown →

Hamburg

Kutztown

Topton

Lebanon

Bernville

Berks

County

Reading

Boyertown

← Harrisburg

Lebanon

Cornwall

Hershey

Mt. Gretna

Hopewell Furnace

Pottstown

Manheim

Ephrata

Lititz

Elizabethtown

Marietta

Intercourse

Lancaster

Downingtown

York

Columbia

Strasburg

Coatesville

Lancaster

County

Quarryville

Longwood Gardens

Jennersville

Philadelphia →

Pennsylvania

Baltimore →

Maryland

Susquehanna River

The Germans didn't concern themselves much with the outside world. While Penn and his heirs bickered over politics, they stayed close to hearth and home, bargained skillfully for the best land, and worked the fertile limestone soil that continues to make this one of the most productive areas in the country. Even the American Revolution left them relatively unfazed. Congress fled to Lancaster for a brief period in 1777, but otherwise the area was spared. In fact, some businesses did quite well, including the ironmongers who supplied the Continental Army with arms and ammunition.

After the war, Lancaster became a gateway to the frontier. Thousands of pioneers headed west on the Philadelphia-Lancaster Turnpike, the nation's first toll road, taking with them the Conestoga wagons and Pennsylvania rifles that were developed in the area and later became symbols of the frontier. Industry was taking root, too, boosted by completion of the Union Canal in 1828 and expansion of the railroad.

A number of famous people emerged. Daniel Boone, that archetype of rugged individualism, was raised in present-day Berks County before his family moved to North Carolina in 1750. F.W. Woolworth established his first successful five-and-dime store in Lancaster in 1879. And the multitalented Robert Fulton,

The Old Order Amish have come to characterize the plain folk of the area.

best known for his steamship *Clermont,* lived and worked in the area, as did political figures like James Buchanan, the 15th President of the United States, and Simon Cameron, Secretary of War under President Abraham Lincoln.

Much has changed, but folks haven't lost sight of tradition. You see it in the family farms and little white churches, the hex signs and carefully tended gardens. Naturally it's a bit more crowded than it used to be. Subdivisions sprawl around the larger towns. Outlet malls and tourist attractions crowd some of the major thoroughfares. And Lancaster County has been named to a list of the hundred most endangered historic treasures by the World Monument Fund, an international preservation organization. But this is still one of the

Much has changed over the years, but many people remain close to the values of rural life.

most bountiful agricultural areas in the country, and most folks have remained close to the values of rural life. They work with their hands, live close to the land, and are committed to family and church. Old Order Amish and Mennonites live much as their ancestors did, shunning electricity, wearing traditional "plain" dress, and traveling in horse-drawn buggies. Members of less conservative groups have a similar commitment to hard work and plain living.

It all makes for a fascinating backdrop to the area's many charms: historic inns, covered bridges, antique and quilt shops, wineries, farmers' markets, and a wide variety of fine dining, from smart little bistros in downtown Lancaster to old-fashioned smorgasbords piled high with homemade sausage, scrapple, dumplings, potato pancakes, shoofly pie and other Pennsylvania German specialties. You can tour an 18th-century cloister in Ephrata; ride a vintage railroad in Strasburg; attend a Renaissance fair near Manheim; stroll through the lovely Moravian town of Lititz; or take in breathtaking vistas along the Susquehanna River.

Within 45 minutes of Amish country is Hershey, Pennsylvania, home of the chocolate-making giant, with a state-of-the-art amusement park, spectacular gardens and other family attractions. In nearby Berks County is Reading, the self-proclaimed "outlet capital of the world," where you'll find dozens of discount stores with bargains in everything from chain saws to fine china. Lebanon and Berks counties have countless acres of rolling fields, country towns, picturesque farms and historic sites like the 19th-century "iron plantation" at Cornwall Furnace. And if that's not enough, Gettysburg, Harrisburg and the Brandywine Valley are only a short drive away.

So, in the kind of language you'll sometimes hear in these parts, "come on over wunst for a wunderful gut time."

Mennonite women at a quilting bee, one of many traditions kept alive by the "plain folk" of the area.

Getting There

Driving is by far the most convenient way to see Pennsylvania Dutch Country. The city of Lancaster is about 70 miles from Philadelphia, 120 miles from Washington, D.C., 235 miles from Pittsburgh and 170 miles from New York.

Several major arteries lead into the area. From most places, the easiest way is to follow the Pennsylvania Turnpike (Interstate 76) to exit 21 and then travel south on Route 222 to Lancaster. From Washington and Baltimore, follow Interstate 83 north to York, then east on Route 30.

A note about driving safely: Drivers should exercise extra caution in Amish country and other rural areas. Slow-moving trucks, tractors, horse-drawn buggies, bicycles and scooters are common throughout the region and extremely difficult to spot at night. Horses are unpredictable and should be given extra space. If you find yourself "stuck" behind an Amish buggy, be patient. Don't honk the horn or rev the engine. Wait until it's safe and legal to pass, and then proceed cautiously, allowing plenty of room between your vehicle and the buggy.

BY AIRPLANE

The nearest airport is **Lancaster Airport,** just north of the city near Lititz. Major airports in the area are **Philadelphia International, Baltimore-Washington International, Harrisburg International** and **Lehigh Valley International.** Taxis and car rentals are available at all.

BY BUS & RAILROAD

Greyhound (800-231-2222) offers daily bus service to the city of Lancaster from surrounding cities, including New York, Philadelphia, Baltimore, Washington and Pittsburgh. Bus service within Lancaster is provided by the **Red Rose Transit Authority** (717-397-4246).

Amtrak (800-872-7245) offers direct service from Philadelphia and New York. Departures from other cities may require connections.

CAR RENTALS

In most cases, you must be at least 21 years old and have a valid driver's license and at least one major credit card to rent a car. Be sure that you are properly insured for both collision and liability; insurance is usually not included in the base rental fee. You may already be insured by your own insurance or credit card company. Be sure to inquire about applicable discounts, including corporate, credit card or frequent-flyer programs.

Cars may be rented at the following locations:

Avis
Lancaster Airport, Lititz, PA
2385D Bernardville Road, Reading, PA
Harrisburg Airport, Middletown, PA
Reservations: 800-831-2847

Enterprise
1573 Manheim Pike, Lancaster, PA
Reservations: 800-325-8007

Hertz
Lancaster Airport, Lititz, PA
625 East Orange Street, Lancaster, PA
Reading Airport, Route 183, Reading, PA
Harrisburg Airport, Middletown, PA
Reservations: 800-654-3131

Landis
4412 Oregon Pike, Brownstown, PA
Reservations: 717-859-5466

National
Liberty Street and Lititz Pike, Lancaster, PA
Reservations: 717-227-7368

When to Visit

Weather in Pennsylvania Dutch Country runs the gamut: hot and steamy in summer, biting cold in winter, pleasant but occasionally rainy in spring, cool and crisp in fall, with spectacular foliage. Summer brings sudden rainstorms, winter is apt to drop some snow, sometimes heavily. Remember, however, that the weather is unpredictable. Unseasonable cold or warm spells are not uncommon. Indian summer sometimes extends balmy weather well into October, and snow can fall as late as March. If in doubt about the weather, dress in layers and peel clothes on or off as conditions dictate.

Dining

The Pennsylvania Dutch are famous for their hearty country cooking. The emphasis here is on fresh ingredients, large portions and simple preparations, with few fancy sauces or spices. A few specialties include chicken pot pie, scrapple, sausage, Lebanon bologna and other smoked meats; German dishes like *schnitz un knepp* (ham and apples with potato dumplings) and pork and sauerkraut; pickled goods like chow chow (relish) and pepper relish; cheese and fresh ice cream, sometimes sold at the same dairy farms where they're made; rich baked goods like shoofly (molasses) pie, sticky buns, whoopie pie (sort of like a cookie sandwich), apple dumplings and dense breads; and an assortment of snacks and sweets like pretzels, potato chips and traditional Pennsylvania German cookies.

In most cases, food at Pennsylvania Dutch restaurants is served in one of two ways: family-style, with heaping platters passed around banquet tables, or an all-you-can-eat smorgasbord. In either case, you won't walk away hungry.

Beyond Pennsylvania Dutch cooking, you'll find a variety of cuisine, from smart bistros and intriguing ethnic eateries to historic country inns. Finer restaurants may be a little pricey, but there are usually nearby alternatives where you can find a filling and inexpensive meal.

Reservations are highly recommended, especially on weekends. Dress at most establishments is casual but neat; check before arriving when possible. Jackets are not required unless noted.

The price guide indicates approximate cost of dinner for one person, excluding beverage, tax and tip. The standard tip is 15%, more for exceptional service or a large party. In some cases, the gratuity may be included in the bill.

Budget $10 or less
Moderate $11–$25
Expensive $26–$40
Very expensive More than $40

For convenience, the following abbreviations are used in restaurant and lodging reviews:

AE American Express
DC Diners Club
Dis Discover
MC MasterCard
V Visa
BYOB Bring your own bottle

Lodging

Lodging in Pennsylvania Dutch Country is quite diverse, ranging from full-service resorts and historic inns to modest guest houses and motels. Wherever you stay, reservations are essential and should be made as far ahead as possible, especially on weekends and during the busy summer season.

BED & BREAKFAST

A popular option, bed-and-breakfast lodgings vary widely in price and atmosphere. Some are grand houses with lavish period decor and luxurious amenities like Jacuzzis and fireplaces. Others are simpler and less expensive – a comfortable room at a working farm, for

example, where kids can try their hands at milking cows, feeding chickens and other chores.

As the name suggests, breakfast is included in the price of lodging. This can range from a basket of muffins and a cup of coffee to a formal gourmet meal. At some inns, guests eat at separate tables. In others, they dine together. A few offer breakfast in your room. Inquire in advance, depending on your need for privacy. You should also ask about bathroom arrangements. Most rooms have a private bath, but it's not uncommon to find a bath shared by two rooms or a private bath located in the hall.

Many bed-and-breakfasts require a minimum stay of two nights on weekends, three nights on holidays. An opening for a single Friday or Sunday may be available, but often they are difficult to find, especially in summer and fall. In almost all cases, smoking and pets are prohibited inside. Some small inns may not be suitable for young children, although most will make special accommodations with advance notice. Most welcome corporate meetings, weddings and other special events, and a few have conference facilities for large groups.

Traveling With Children

Pennsylvania Dutch Country is a great place to travel with kids. There's an abundance of family lodging and dining, and plenty of attractions that both children and adults will find interesting (see "Kid Stuff" in "Ten Great Getaways" for specific ideas). Resorts and farm houses are fun places to base your family for a few days, offering all sorts of diversions when you tire of the usual hot spots. For meals, the various smorgasbords are a good choice. Kids can choose whatever they like, and the atmosphere tends to be fun and informal.

Behave Yourself!

Visiting Amish country requires a bit of cultural sensitivity and plain good manners. Remember, this isn't a theme park but a real community. Certain boundaries need to be respected.

First and most important, Amish folk prohibit the making of "graven images," including photographs. Do not attempt to photograph or videotape Amish

An Amish elder at a public sale.

people. If you must take pictures, do so at a distance and only in public places. Do not trespass on private property or approach Amish schools. If you're a serious or professional photographer, talk to your subjects first, let them get to know you, and acquire permission before you start shooting.

These are gentle people. Overly assertive behavior is inappropriate. Don't gawk, ask rude questions or use profanity. Remember, too, that the Amish are not accustomed to brief clothing; it's best to cover up bare shoulders and avoid wearing skimpy shorts.

Additional Information

TOURIST CENTERS

Hershey Information Center
Hershey, PA 17033.
Tel: 717-534-3005.

Lebanon Valley Tourist and Visitors Bureau
Quality Inn, 6254 Quentin Road,
Lebanon, PA 17042.
Tel: 717-272-8555.

Mennonite Information Center
2209 Millstream Road, Lancaster,
PA 17602-1494. Tel: 717-299-0954.

Pennsylvania Dutch Convention and Visitors Bureau
501 Greenfield Road, Lancaster,
PA 17601. Tel: 717-299-8901 or
toll-free 800-723-8824.

Pennsylvania Travel
Pennsylvania Department of
Commerce, Harrisburg, PA 17101.
Tel: 717-255-3252.

Reading and Berks County Visitors Bureau
VF Factory Outlet, Park Road
and Hill Avenue, P.O. Box 6677,
Reading, PA 19610. Tel: 610-375-
4085 or toll-free 800-443-6610.

Southern Market Downtown Visitors Center
100 South Queen Street,
Lancaster, PA 17603.
Tel: 717-397-3531.

Strasburg Information Center
Historic Strasburg Inn,
Route 896, Strasburg, PA 17579.
Tel: 717-687-7922.

Susquehanna Heritage Tourist and Information Center
445 Linden Street, Columbia, PA
17512. Tel: 717-684-5249.

OUTDOOR RECREATION

Berks County Parks and Recreation Department
2083 Tulpehocken Road,
Wyomissing, PA 19610.
Tel: 610-372-8939.

Lancaster County Department of Parks and Recreation
1050 Rockford Road, Lancaster,
PA 17602. Tel: 717-299-8215.

Pennsylvania Bureau of State Parks
P.O. Box 8551, Harrisburg, PA
17105-8551. Tel: 717-675-1121.

Pennsylvania Fish Commission
P.O. Box 1673, Harrisburg, PA
17105-1673. Tel: 717-657-4518.

Pennsylvania Game Commission
2001 Elmerton Avenue,
Harrisburg, PA 17110-9797.
Tel: 717-787-4250.

Who Are The Amish?

*T*he Amish are caught in a dilemma. They regard themselves as a people apart, but the more they try to separate themselves from the outside world, the more they attract attention.

These are the "gentle people" of pacifism and personal humility, who baffle the outside world with their tenacious hold on the past and strict code of behavior. They forgo electricity, farm with horses, shun higher education, and forbid the ownership of cars. And of course they wear traditional "plain" clothing – dark suits and black or straw hats for men, long dresses and head coverings of solid colors for women.

The Amish emphasize traditional values and practices, but they are also masters of compromise. They cunningly balance convenience against tradition and make delicate bargains that embrace enough of the modern world to give them prosperity while rejecting those aspects likely to threaten the integrity of their family life.

Lancaster County's 20,000 Old Order Amish are loosely linked to nearly a thousand other congregations in the United States and Canada. Their religious roots

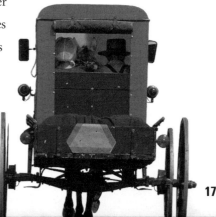

Amish children dress much as adults do; "plain" clothing is an expression of personal humility and heightens group identity.

stretch back to the 16th-century Anabaptists who parted ways with the Protestant Reformation in 1525 in Switzerland. Adhering to the literal teachings of Jesus, the Anabaptists emphasized obedience to God's will, adult baptism, pacifism, the separation of church and state, and a disciplined church community distinct from the larger world. They were dubbed rebaptizers, or Anabaptists, because they insisted on baptizing adults who had already gone through the ritual as infants. Because adult baptism was considered both a heresy and a political threat, it triggered severe persecution. Thousands of Anabaptists were drowned, decapitated or burned at the stake for their beliefs.

Persecuted in Europe, the Amish emphasize separation from mainstream culture, believing that they are called on to be a peculiar people.

The Amish splintered off from the Swiss Anabaptists in 1693 under the leadership of Jacob Ammann, from whom they take their name. Hutterites, Mennonites and some Brethren groups also trace their lineage to the Anabaptists. The Amish share basic religious beliefs with other Christians but put special emphasis on simplicity, community, obedience, humility, mutual aid and separation from the world, a way of life galvanized by the persecution they suffered in Europe.

The Amish are flourishing in North America. From a small band of about 5,000 at the turn of the century, they have grown to more than 150,000. In addition to a high birth rate, the Amish have constructed a variety of "social fences" to protect themselves from the turbulence of modern life.

The Amish emphasize small-scale values. The Lancaster community revolves around a hundred church districts consisting of 25 to 35 families. Worship services, held every other Sunday, rotate from home to home because the Amish have no churches.

Farms and businesses are also relatively small. Large operations employing more than a dozen people are thought to lead to arrogance and wealth that would disturb the relative equality of Amish life. The virtues of humility and simplicity also stress a smallness of ego, which promotes cooperation within the community.

Social control also separates the Amish from the outside world. Obedience is considered a virtue. Children learn at an early age to obey parents, teachers and elders. At baptism, in the late teens and early twenties, young adults promise to obey the *ordnung* – the discipline of the community passed from generation to generation by word of mouth. It prescribes the use of horses and traditional dress, and forbids high school, cars, television, electricity, and portraits or photographs, among other things. It also clarifies the importance of the community over individual whims and wishes.

The bishop of each church district interprets and enforces the ordnung. Bishops gather periodically to coordinate activities

Harvest time at an Amish farm. Tractors with rubber tires are forbidden in the field.

Acts of mutual aid, such as this barn-raising, are considered a duty among the Amish.

and discuss troublesome issues such as the use of computers, eating in restaurants and embryo transplants in cattle. Individuals who violate community norms are asked to make a public confession in the church service. If they refuse, they are liable for excommunication or social avoidance, known as shunning.

Amish education is another barrier around the community. Eight years of school is considered to be adequate for a successful life in the Amish community. After many legal battles, the U.S.

Supreme Court in 1972 declared that Amish students could terminate their formal education at the eighth grade. Today, Amish youngsters attend one-room schools operated by Amish parents. The curriculum stresses practical skills but does not include science or religion. Indeed, religion is not formally taught in any sector of Amish society, including the church. Religious values are taught by example, not by formal doctrine.

Other rules regulate interaction with outsiders. Once burned by the fires of persecution, the Amish emphasize separation from mainstream culture, believing that they are called out from the world to be a peculiar people. Although the Amish speak English, their Pennsylvania German dialect heightens group identity and stifles contact with outsiders. The taboo on car ownership impedes mobility. The shunning of telephones, television, radio and other types of mass media in their homes limits contamination by foreign values. Avoiding public organizations and political affairs also helps draw boundaries with the surrounding world.

But the Amish are also capable of striking bargains with the larger culture. These compromises often seem like riddles or contradictions. Pragmatism permits the use and hiring of motor vehicles, for example, because it bolsters their economic well-being – but not the ownership or driving of vehicles, since such mobility would erode the integrity of the community. For similar reasons, telephones are acceptable in shops or barns but not in homes.

True happiness, the Amish say, comes from a stable community. They discover themselves only when they yield to tradition.

Amish farmers typically use tractors around their barns for heavy-duty jobs such as powering feed grinders and hydraulic systems. In the fields, however, modern farm machinery is pulled by horses. This distinction preserves work for Amish children and protects the horse, which has become an important symbol of Amish identity. Twelve-volt batteries are used to stir milk in bulk tanks, but tapping into 110-volt power lines is forbidden – largely because this would bring into Amish homes the secular values transmitted by radio and television and a variety of modern gadgets that would undermine the simplicity of Amish life.

The complexities don't stop there. Synthetic materials that require no ironing are used to make their "plain" clothes. Carriages made in Amish shops from fiberglass and vinyl conform to customary colors and styles. Newer Amish homes are remarkably contemporary with modern kitchens, bathrooms and gas appliances. But washing machines and sometimes sewing machines and cake mixers are powered by hydraulic pressure.

The Amish of Lancaster County are among the most progressive in North America, and infringements of the rules are sometimes treated leniently. A young farmer is given six months to replace the rubber tires on his tractor with steel wheels. A businessman is allowed several months to complete a project before getting rid of his illicit computer.

The Amish are caught in a demographic crisis – too many people and too few acres.

But the forces of urbanization and industrialization have squeezed Lancaster's Amish relentlessly. Shrinking farmland, sharply rising land prices, and their own growing population have created a demographic crisis – too many Amish and too few acres.

To cope with the pressures, some families migrate to more rural areas. And whenever possible, farms are subdivided into smaller operations. But these moves are not enough, and the Amish face the big question: Would they leave their farms for factories? Once again, they compromise. Yes, they would leave the plow behind, but not for factory work, which they believe erodes the stability of family life. "The lunch pail," said one bishop, "is the biggest threat to our way of life." Cottage industries offered a way around the impasse. By starting small businesses, the

Amish earn a living surrounded by family and friends. Today, nearly half of Lancaster's Amish are employed in manufacturing a variety of crafts, equipment, quilts and cabinetry.

For the moment at least, the cottage industries are a happy compromise. They allow members of the community to leave their plows but stay close to ancestral roots. But even these small shops pose a danger to Amish society. They place Amish entrepreneurs in frequent contact with outsiders and are introducing a three-tier class system – farmers, day laborers and businessmen – which in the long run could ruin the equality of Amish society.

The cost of being Amish is high, but there are benefits in return – virtually no divorce, fewer trips to the psychiatrist's office, lower rates of suicide, few drug and alcohol problems, no dependency on public welfare, and less environmental damage. Amish life offers a distinct sense of meaning and identity, a rare commodity these days.

These virtues require major concessions – forgoing unbridled individualism, giving up the pursuit of pleasure and convenience. But the Amish argue that true happiness and personal satisfaction are woven into the very fabric of a stable community, and that they discover themselves as individuals only when they yield to the wisdom of tradition.

HIGHLIGHTS

- Villages of Intercourse and Bird-in-Hand
- People's Place
- Gordonville Auction
- Factory outlets

Amish Heartland

*T*ravelers in Amish country are faced with a stark contrast between the simple life of the Plain People and the flamboyant commercialism of the tourist trade. Two main thoroughfares – Routes 30 and 340 – are particularly congested. About 5 million tourists travel these corridors each year, pouring money into the motels, restaurants, outlet stores and "genuine" Amish attractions that crowd the roadside.

But even here, you're never more than five or 10 minutes from the family farms and workshops that are the real heartland of Amish life. They're not difficult to find. Just point the car down any back road and you're bound to hear the whir of Amish buggies or find Amish farmers working their fields with a team of horses.

Want to meet them? Perhaps the best way is to stop wherever you see a sign advertising produce, quilts, handmade furniture or other crafts. Public auctions and farmers' markets are good places too. The **Gordonville Fire Company Auction** in March is a raucous, colorful event, as is the **Green Dragon Farmers' Market** on Friday in Ephrata. You may also inquire at the

Amish boys get a bird's-eye view of the Gordonville Auction. Right, Amish quilt.

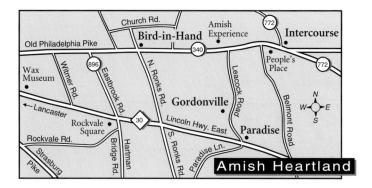

Amish Heartland

Pennsylvania Dutch Convention and Visitors Bureau (Route 30 and Greenfield Road) about arranging a special tour of an Amish farm or dinner with an Amish or Mennonite family. Remember, Old Order Amish don't usually permit themselves to be photographed by strangers, so leave the camera in the car.

For more details about Amish life, visit the **People's Place** in the busy little village of **Intercourse** on Route 340. The oft-punned name was probably taken from an old racetrack known as the Entercourse, or perhaps from the intercourse of Old Kings Highway and the Wilmington-Erie Railroad. In any case, you'll find plenty of gift shops catering to tourists, including a shopping complex known as **Kitchen Kettle Village** and the **Intercourse Pretzel Factory**, where you can try twisting pretzel dough on a free tour of the factory.

Exhibits at the People's Place include an informative slide show and feature film that explore the Amish, Mennonite and Hutterite people, and a museum, Amish World, with a fascinating collection of folk art and clever interactive displays especially designed for kids. A book shop and craft store on the first floor are quite interesting, too.

Another good source of information is the **Mennonite Information Center** just off Route 30, where exhibits include a 20-

minute film about the Amish and Mennonites and a reproduction of the Hebrew Tabernacle. Mennonite guides are available to join you for back road tours of Amish farmland and personal reflections on Pennsylvania Dutch culture.

There are several other attractions related to the Amish, although most are more commercial in nature. About a mile west of Intercourse on Route 340, for example, is the **Amish Country Homestead**, a nine-room replica of an Old Order Amish house. Visitors learn about traditional Amish dress, unique furnishings and church services. Here also is the **Amish Experience F/X Theater**, a high-tech, multi-screen presentation of the Plain People's turbulent history told from an Amish boy's perspective. Nearby is the **Weavertown One-Room Schoolhouse**, a century-old building with original desks, bell and blackboard now inhabited by animated wax figures.

About five miles east on busy Route 30 is the 10-room **Amish Farm and House**, dating to 1805, which features a 35-minute tour explaining the Plain People's way of life. A series of dioramas at the nearby **Wax Museum of Lancaster County Heritage** chronicles local history from the arrival of various Anabaptists in the early 1700s to the Civil War. A few minutes away, **Historic Mill Bridge Village** offers a glimpse of early life with an 1812 farmhouse, an 18th-century gristmill and a covered bridge. Buggy rides are available, and a variety of craftsmen demonstrate blacksmithing, broom making, quilting and other crafts.

The Old Order Amish live much as their ancestors did, shunning electricity, wearing "plain" dress, and traveling in horse-drawn buggies.

Other attractions in the area include the **American Music Theater**, which presents musical revues with a professional cast and live orchestra, and **Dutch Wonderland**, an amusement park with 44 acres of rides, shows and gardens. The little village of **Bird-in-Hand** is also very popular, with a busy farmers' market, a variety of craft and gift shops, and the **Old Village Store**, one of the oldest hardware stores in the country. The town was established in the 1730s during the construction of the Old Philadelphia Pike and was named after a local inn.

It may seem ironic, considering the Amish community's rejection of modern consumerism, but the area is also home to dozens of factory outlets. Most are at the **Tanger Outlet Center** and **Rockvale Square Outlets** on Route 30, both with deep discounts on everything from frying pans to designer underwear.

The Amish rely on horses for farm work and transportation and regard them as a symbol of their traditional way of life.

Where to Stay

Bird-in-Hand Family Inn

2740 Old Philadelphia Pike (Route 340), Bird-in-Hand, PA 17505.
Tel: 717-768-8271 or toll-free 800-537-2535. Fax: 717-768-1117.

This family-friendly motel offers basic but comfortable accommodations within minutes of popular tourist attractions. Ask for a room in the rear building for reduced traffic noise and proximity to the pools. *Rates: $49–$90 double occupancy. Children 16 and under stay free; no pets. Amenities: 100 rooms with private bath, air conditioning, telephones, cable television. Indoor and outdoor pools, hot tub, tennis and basketball courts, game room, meeting rooms. Free bus tour of Amish country. Adjacent restaurant; ask about bed-and-breakfast packages; gift shop, parking. All major credit cards.*

Churchtown Inn

2100 Main Street (Route 23), Churchtown, PA 17555.
Tel: 717-445-7794 or toll-free 800-637-4446.

Travelers who like theme weekends and other social activities will find this friendly bed-and-breakfast a special treat. Events include Murder Mystery and Mother Daughter weekends, demonstrations of Amish cooking, an evening of New Orleans Jazz, a Thanksgiving feast, and a black-tie Victorian ball. It's not uncommon to hear one of the guests or innkeepers play a selection of favorite tunes on the baby-grand piano in the parlor even when there are no special happenings. There are weekends dedicated to peace and quiet, too. Set close to the road in the heart of tiny Churchtown, the house is built of fieldstone in a combination of Federal and Edwardian styles. The oldest section dates to 1735, with major additions from the early 1800s. Guest rooms are comfortably furnished; several are dressed in shades of pink and violet with carpet, sheer curtains, Amish quilts and perhaps a canopy or antique sleigh bed, armoire and marble-top vanity. The attached carriage house is the largest and most lavishly decorated. Some rooms on the third floor are smaller, with sloped ceilings. Common rooms include a homey den and formal Victorian parlor. A five-course breakfast is served on Royal Doulton china in a sun room with views of a lovely patio and garden. Dinner with an Amish family is available Saturday evening and select weeknights with advance notice. Surrey rides are available on weekends, weather permitting. *Rates: $55–$135 double occupancy; two-night minimum on weekends, three-night minimum on holidays and special weekends. Children 12 years and older are welcome; no pets. Amenities: 10 rooms with air conditioning; nine rooms with private baths. Full schedule of special events. Garden, patio, parking. MC, V.*

⭐ Creekside Inn

44 Leacock Road, Paradise, PA 17562. Tel: 717-687-0333. Fax: 717-687-8200.

Built in 1781 by David Witmer, a prominent miller, farmer and entrepreneur and friend of George Washington, this handsome limestone mansion is set on two peaceful acres of lawn and woods on Pequea Creek just a few minutes from Route 30. A tasteful marriage of contemporary and antique furnishings complement the house's solid rustic architecture. There are wide-plank floors, thick plaster walls with recessed windows, a coal stove in one of the dining rooms, and a big stone hearth in the living room, where innkeepers Dennis and Cathy Zimmermann keep an interesting collection of glass communion sets made in Czechoslovakia. Guest rooms range in size from snug to spacious. The two largest have queen-sized four-poster beds, limestone fireplaces, wood floors and perhaps an antique dresser and writing desk; the first-floor suite has two bedrooms with an additional double brass bed. A full country breakfast of homemade bread, fruit crisp, shoofly pie, Lancaster ham and sausage, and hot dishes like cinnamon raisin French toast, quiche, and pineapple ham and eggs are served in two dining rooms. Guests are invited to lounge on the porch or swinging bench, stroll through the large herb and vegetable garden, or try fishing in the creek, which is stocked with trout and bass. Dinner with an Amish family

⭐ indicates a personal favorite of the author

can be arranged with advance notice. *Rates: $75–$105 double occupancy; two-night minimum on select weekends. Limited availability for children; no pets. Amenities: Five rooms with private bath and air conditioning, including a two-bedroom suite. Garden, porch, parking. Dis, MC, V.*

Fassitt Mansion

6051 Old Philadelphia Pike (Route 340), Gap, PA 17527. Tel: 717-442-3139 or toll-free 800-653-3141. Fax: 717-442-9179.

Surrounded by farmland about 10 minutes east of Intercourse, this extraordinary white stucco house was constructed in 1717 and completely rebuilt in 1845. Guests have the run of the entire place, including a full kitchen, dining room and living room, with 12-foot ceilings, wide-plank floors, heavy woodwork, thick stucco walls and gas fireplace. The decor has an open rustic feeling, nicely offset with antiques collected and refinished by innkeeper Bill Collins. Ask him to show you one of the hidden rooms, originally built to stash valuables and later used to hide runaway slaves on the Underground Railroad. Four second-floor bedrooms – all with 10-foot ceilings and stenciled plank floors – are furnished with a combination of antiques and reproductions, quilts, lace curtains, arm chairs and sofas. A fifth room – usually saved for walk-ins – is on the first floor, just off the foyer. Two rooms have gas fireplaces. A library and common room are on the third floor, where guests are invited to leave a few words on the corridor wall – a unique traveler's chronicle. A hearty country breakfast of fruit, cheese, eggs, two kinds of sausage, pancakes or waffles is served at a 12-foot-long table in the dining room. Guests are always welcome to help themselves to refreshments and homemade apple pie in the kitchen, or gather around an open fire in the backyard for a marshmallow roast. *Rates: $75–$115 double occupancy. No pets or children. Amenities: Five rooms with private bath (one in corridor) and air conditioning, two with fireplace. Garden, porch, parking. MC, V.*

Flowers & Thyme
238 Strasburg Pike, Lancaster, PA 17602. Tel: 717-393-1460. Fax: 717-399-1986.

A profusion of flowers and abundant greenery surround this trim little bed-and-breakfast about a mile south of Route 30. Built by an Amishman in 1941, the house has three guest rooms on the second floor ranging in size from small to moderate. The Garden Room, for example, is snug but pretty, with a queen-sized brass bed, floral wallpaper, lace curtains and a gas fireplace. The more spacious Thyme Room offers a Shaker-style, four-poster bed with floral comforter, antique dressers, and a large bathroom with Jacuzzi and stall shower. Common rooms include a living room and parlor with wood floors and comfortable contemporary furnishings. Breakfast is served in an airy, skylit dining room that opens to a brick patio overlooking the garden and neighboring farm. Entrees include omelettes, waffles and fruit, French toast with berry sauce, potato quiche

and more. Dinner with an Amish family can be arranged upon request. *Rates: $80–$100 double occupancy; two-night minimum on holidays. Children over 12 are welcome at all times; children over two are welcome weekdays only; no pets. Amenities: three rooms with private bath and air conditioning; one room with Jacuzzi, another with gas fireplace. Patio, garden, parking. MC, V.*

Fulton Steamboat Inn
P.O. Box 333, Routes 30 and 896, Strasburg, PA 17579. Tel: 717-299-9999 or toll-free 800-922-2229.

Named after Robert Fulton, the Lancaster native credited with inventing the steamship, this novel three-story hotel is decked out like a Mississippi paddle boat inside and out. There are three basic room categories. Accommodations on the first floor or "promenade deck" feature queen-sized and bunk beds. Rooms on the second floor or "observation deck" have queen-sized beds and a sitting area. And the third floor or "sun deck" has oversized rooms with a choice of two queen-sized beds or a king-sized bed, a small private balcony, and whirlpool bath. All rooms are comfortably furnished with plush carpet, television, microwave, mini-refrigerator and a few nautical touches. The hotel is located next to the Rockvale Square Outlets and minutes away from other Route 30 attractions. Ask about dining and lodging packages. *Rates: $50–$135 double occupancy; two-night minimum preferred on weekends; three-night minimum preferred on holidays. Wheelchair-accessible; children* are welcome; no pets. *Amenities: 96 rooms with private bath, air conditioning, cable television and telephone; some rooms with whirlpool tub. Indoor pool and Jacuzzi, fitness room, game room, gift shop, bake shop, restaurant and lounge, banquet and conference facilities accommodating up to 80 people, parking. AE, Dis, MC, V.*

Greystone Manor
2658 Old Philadelphia Pike,
Bird-in-Hand, PA 17505.
Tel: 717-393-4233.

Mounds of summer lilies and black-eyed Susans greet you at the entrance of this large brick inn capped with a mansard roof and rounded dormers. The structure was originally built in the mid-19th century as a farmhouse and was refashioned later in Victorian style. Spacious common rooms feature high ceilings, wood floors, tall windows draped with lace curtains, and Victorian-style furniture. Breakfast is served at three tables in a handsome dining room and may include dishes like quiche Lorraine, frittatas, oven pancakes or stuffed French bread. There are 13 guest rooms in all, including several two-room suites. The largest and most elaborately furnished are on the first and second floors of the main house, some with plank floors, four-poster or canopy beds, stained-glass windows, sitting areas, an assortment of antiques and large, well-equipped bathrooms. Three rooms tucked under the eaves on the third floor are small, pretty and private, and there are another six rooms – including a two-room suite – in the carriage house out back. *Rates: $70–$135*

double occupancy; two-night minimum on weekends, three-night minimum on holidays. Children are welcome in the carriage house; no pets. Amenities: 13 rooms (including several two-room suites) with private bath, cable television and air conditioning. Patio, garden, parking. MC, V.*

Holiday Inn Lancaster Host Hotel
2300 Lincoln Highway (Route 30),
Lancaster, PA 17602.
Tel: 717-299-5500 or toll-free
800-233-0121. Fax: 717-295-5112.

Popular with families and business travelers, this full-service resort hotel sprawls across 220 acres near outlet centers and other Route 30 attractions. Standard rooms have a king-sized bed or two queen-sized beds, some with pool or golf-course view. A few two-room suites have a king-sized bed and sitting area with pullout sofa. Recreational facilities include a 27-hole golf course, indoor and outdoor pools and tennis courts, two restaurants and nightclub. A supervised children's program is offered in summer. *Rates: $99–$159 double occupancy; two-night minimum on select weekends and holidays. Children are welcome; wheelchair-accessible; no pets. Amenities: 330 rooms with private bath, air conditioning, telephone and cable television. Indoor and outdoor pools and tennis courts, whirlpool, 27-hole golf course, driving range and miniature golf; basketball and volleyball courts, fitness room, game room, playground, bicycle rental, jogging and biking trail. Two restaurants, nightclub, banquet, conference and exhibition facilities. Patio, parking. All major credit cards.*

✦ Inn at Twin Linden
2092 Main Street (Route 23),
Churchtown, PA 17555.
Tel: 717-445-7619. Fax: 717-445-4656.

Innkeepers Donna and Robert Leahy have brought a sophisticated blend of traditional and contemporary styles to this extraordinary inn, built in the mid-19th century as a private home for the daughter of a prominent ironmaster. The Palladian Suite is particularly stunning. Named after the bank of arched windows overlooking a tableau of Amish barns, silos and cornfields, and decorated in soothing shades of tan and white, the well-designed room manages to feel open and airy despite relatively low ceilings. A skylight, pellet-burning stove, CD player and two-person Jacuzzi add to the atmosphere of indulgence. The same artful touch is evident in other rooms, ranging in size from cozy to spacious, most with Shaker-style queen-sized beds. A bathroom skylight in the Cottage Room, for example, adds a welcome sense of space to an otherwise snug fit. The much larger Linden and Sarah Jenkins rooms, both with canopy beds, are furnished with impeccable taste; the latter has a fireplace and Jacuzzi. Guests are welcome to snuggle fireside on a plump sofa in the parlor, or soak in the outdoor whirlpool and listen to the clip-clop of Amish buggies. In the morning, a gourmet breakfast is served in the plank-floor dining room or on a lovely brick patio surrounded by a profusion of herbs, flowers and ancient trees, including the eponymous linden trees. The menu changes daily but may include a few dishes from Donna's gourmet cookbook – grilled polenta in dill cream sauce, croissant cinnamon raisin buns, pesto eggs with leeks and asparagus, or walnut French toast with

Amish children attend one-room schoolhouses. Education is limited to eight years. High school is not permitted.

poached pears. Inspired candle-light dining is available on Saturday evening as well (see "Where to Eat"). *Rates: $100–$210 double occupancy; two-night minimum on weekends and holidays. Children are welcome on weeknights; no pets. Amenities: seven rooms with private bath, air conditioning and cable television; several rooms with fireplace, Jacuzzi and/or video. Outdoor whirlpool, garden, patio, gift shop, parking. Fixed-price dinner Saturday. AE, Dis, MC, V.*

Parson's Place in Paradise
37 Leacock Road, Paradise, PA 17562. Tel: 717-687-8529.

Set on Pequea Creek in the heart of Amish country, this snug limestone house was built in 1754 by the prominent Feree family and was later occupied by the well-known Park Seed Company. Today, the house is an attractive bed-and-breakfast surrounded by well-tended gardens. Three cozy rooms are comfortably furnished with quilt-covered queen-sized or twin beds, a collection of antiques, and the thick stone-and-plaster walls and recessed windows typical of the period. Two rooms with a shared bath may be rented individually or as a two-bedroom suite. A full breakfast is served in a new sun room with views of the back garden and patio or by the old-fashioned fireplace in the living room. Dinner with an Amish family can be arranged with advance notice. *Rates: $50–$80 double occupancy. Children and pets are welcome with advance notice. Amenities: Three rooms with air conditioning, two with shared bath. Patio, garden, parking. MC, V.*

Village Inn of Bird-in-Hand
P.O. Box 253, 2695 Old Philadelphia Pike, Bird-in-Hand, PA 17505. Tel: 717-293-8369 or toll-free 800-914-2473. Fax: 717-768-1117.

The inn has had various incar-nations over the decades. The earliest was a crude log cabin built about 1734 to shelter surveyors working on the Old Philadelphia Pike. The present hotel – a handsome brick structure fronted by a two-story veranda – dates to 1852, although part of the foundation remains from the first building. Listed on the National Register of Historic Places, the inn now offers 11 rooms decorated in country Victorian style with a few thoughtful contemporary touches. The real stars here are the large suites. The McNabb Room, for example, is decked out in Kelly green drapes and floral wallpaper, a king-sized four-poster bed, gas fireplace and two-person Jacuzzi. The second-floor Groff Suite is equally impressive, with a king-sized bed, wood-burning stove and cathedral ceiling. The smaller rooms are quite pleasing, too. A generous Continental breakfast is served in a pretty sun room with wood floors and wicker tables. A complimentary bus tour of Lancaster County is offered daily except Sunday. Ask about lodging and dining packages. *Rates: $99–$129 double occupancy. No charge for children three and under; no pets. Ameni-ties: 11 rooms with private bath, air conditioning, telephone and cable television; one room with fireplace and Jacuzzi; one room with wood-burning stove. Free bus tour; use of pool, tennis courts and other recreational facilities at* *nearby Bird-in-Hand Family Inn. Parking. AE, Dis, MC, V.*

C A M P I N G

Red Run Campground
877 Martin Church Road, New Holland, PA 17557. Tel: 717-445-4526.

More than 100 sites, many with full hookups, as well as picnic tables, barbecue, grocery store and lake.

Roamer's Retreat Campground
5005 Lincoln Highway East (Route 30), Kinzer, PA 17535. Tel: 717-442-4287.

About 100 sites with play-ground, game room, grocery store and special activities.

Spring Gulch Resort Campground
475 Lynch Road, New Holland, PA 17557. Tel: 717-354-3100 or toll-free 800-255-5744.

More than 450 sites for tents, mobile homes and cabins on 115 acres, with pool, lake, playground, bathhouse, tennis courts and more.

Where to Eat

Bird-in-Hand Family Restaurant
2760 Old Philadelphia Pike, Bird-in-Hand, PA 17505. Tel: 717-768-8266.

There are no tricks here, just plentiful country cooking in a casual family atmosphere.

Tourists vie for space with local folks who come for generous helpings of roast beef and turkey drenched in gravy, chicken pot pie, chicken corn soup and other Dutch specialties. All-you-can-eat buffets (Thu–Sat evening) are a good deal for big appetites. The nearby Bird-in-Hand Bakery whips up an assortment of calorie-packed desserts – wet bottom shoofly pie, apple dumplings, buns, cookies and cakes. *Budget–moderate. Mon–Sat 6am–8pm. No reservations. MC, V.*

Good 'n Plenty
East Brook Road (Route 896) Smoketown, PA 17576. Tel: 717-394-7111.

This large, spirited restaurant offers classic Pennsylvania Dutch specialties in an old Amish farm-house built in 1871. It's sort of like a family dinner for about 600 or so. Diners are served family-style at long tables with a dozen or so people at each. The meal starts with soup or salad and then pushes on to round after round of rib-sticking favorites – huge bowls of mashed potatoes, pitchers of gravy, and oversized platters of fried chicken, pork and sauerkraut, ham, meat loaf, turkey, noodles, homemade bread and more. And just when you think you can't eat another bite, they start on dessert – pie, ice cream, cake, cookies. One price covers every-thing. Only big eaters need apply. *Moderate. Mon–Sat 11:30am–8pm. Reservations for bus groups only. MC, V.*

An Amish boy dashes down a country lane outside Leola.

☆ Inn at Twin Linden
2092 Main Street (Route 23),
Churchtown, PA 17555.
Tel: 717-445-7619.

A sumptuous, four-course, fixed-price dinner is served on Saturday in an intimate candlelit dining area overlooking the garden at this charming 19th-century inn. A creative matching of fresh, artfully prepared ingredients is the hallmark of owner and chef Donna Leahy. The menu changes every week, but a few highlights might include wild mushroom consommé with truffles, seared foie gras with ginger, apple and apricot, Maine lobster tart with chanterelles, chives and chevre mashed potatoes, and rack of lamb with caramelized onions and rosemary pesto. Desserts like lemon mascarpone mousse with raspberries or fresh peach cobbler with homemade cinnamon gelato are equally tempting. It's pricey but worth it – a fine choice for a special occasion. *Expensive. Saturday seatings at 6:30pm, 7:15pm and 8pm. BYOB. Reservations required. AE, Dis, MC, V.*

Kling House

Kitchen Kettle Village,
Route 772, Intercourse PA 17534.
Tel: 717-768-7300.

When weather allows, diners sometimes lounge on the porch and watch Amish buggies pass by, much as Pat Burnley, the owner of this pleasant, family-friendly restaurant, did as a child. Mrs. Burnley grew up in the house – now the restaurant – that anchors the western edge of Kitchen Kettle Village, a collection of quaint shops and galleries in the middle of old Intercourse village. Before heading for the shops, start your day with a breakfast of peach melba pancakes or maple cinnamon French toast, both made with Kitchen Kettle products. Dinner may include raspberry chicken, tuna with a sauce of mint jelly, or traditional *schnitz un knepp* (ham and apples with potato dumplings). While you're waiting for your meal, you can nibble on crackers with cream cheese and Kitchen Kettle's pepper jam. *Moderate. Breakfast Mon–Sat 8am–11am; lunch 11am–4pm; dinner Apr–Dec Thu–Sat 4pm–8pm. No alcohol. Reservations recommended. Dis, MC, V.*

Lemon Grass Thai Restaurant

2481 Lincoln Highway East
(Route 30), Lancaster, PA 17602.
Tel: 717-295-1621.

A Thai restaurant in Amish Country? Well, yes and no. Located on busy Route 30 across from Rockvale Square, this lovely little place features Thai specialties bursting with a tangy mix of garlic, chili pepper, cilantro, tamarind, basil, curry and mint. Standards such as satay (paper-thin grilled pork with peanut sauce) and pad Thai (stir-fried noodles with shrimp, hot pepper and peanut sauce) are complemented by less familiar choices, including many vegetarian dishes. And everything is presented with such color and style that it's almost too beautiful to eat. Thai music helps set a restful and somewhat exotic mood which, considering the location, is really quite a feat. *Moderate. Lunch daily 11:30am–3pm, dinner Sun–Thu 3pm– 10pm, Fri–Sat 3pm–11pm. BYOB. Reservations recommended. AE, Dis, MC, V.*

✵ Log Cabin

11 Lehoy Forest Drive, Leola, PA 17540. Tel: 717-626-1181.

Set in the woods near the Rose Hill covered bridge, this former speakeasy now offers a warren of intimate dining rooms – including the original log cabin – with exposed beams, fireplaces, chandeliers, comfy armchairs and a collection of antique paintings. The menu doesn't bow to fashion, concentrating instead on classic Continental cuisine – grilled Norwegian salmon, prime sirloin, shrimp scampi, double-cut lamb chops, chicken rosemary – all extremely well-prepared from the finest ingredients available. Appetizers include smoked trout, onion soup and clams Provençal. The wine list features a thoughtful collection of California labels. The restaurant is somewhat difficult to find, but is well worth searching out. *Expensive. Dinner Mon–Sat 5pm–10pm, Sun 4pm–9pm. Bar and wine list. Reservations preferred. AE, DC, MC, V.*

Miller's Smorgasbord
2811 Lincoln Highway (Route 30), Ronks, PA 17572. Tel: 717-687-8853.

Hungry? You can eat all you like at this huge, fixed-price buffet. Breakfast features fresh fruit, made-to-order omelettes and eggs, French toast, pancakes, pan-fried scrapple, sausage and more. Dinner is equally substantial, with country favorites like chicken corn soup, slow-roasted beef, turkey, ham, chilled shrimp and chicken pot pie. Leave room for dessert, including chocolate mousse cheesecake, bread pudding and traditional shoofly, pecan and apple pie. In all, there are more than 75 items to choose from. Gift shops and a bakery are also on the premises. A solid choice for families. *Moderate. Breakfast daily Jun–Oct 7am– noon, Sat–Sun Nov–May 7am– noon; dinner daily noon–8pm. Reservations recommended. AE, Dis, MC, V.*

Plain & Fancy Farm
3121 Old Philadelphia Pike (Route 340), Bird-in-Hand, PA 17504. Tel: 717-768-4400.

Hearty, country cooking and lots of it is what you'll find at this all-you-can-eat, family-style restaurant in a complex of shops and attractions (including the Amish Experience F/X Theater) just outside the village of Bird-in-Hand. Customers are seated together at large tables and pass around heaping plates of roast beef, fried chicken, chicken pot pie, sausage, vegetables, mashed potatoes, desserts and more – a lot more. This clearly is not the place for an intimate, candlelit dinner, but gregarious travelers with a taste for old-fashioned comfort food are sure to have a good time. *Moderate. Mon–Thu 11:30am–7pm, Fri–Sat 11:30am– 8pm, Sun noon–6pm; extended summer hours. Reservations recommended. All major credit cards.*

Revere Tavern
3063 Lincoln Highway, Paradise, PA 17562. Tel: 717-687-8601.

Built as a tavern in 1740, this old stone building later served as the home of the Rev. Edward V. Buchanan and his wife Eliza. Her brother was songwriter Stephen Foster, composer of such classic American tunes as "O Susannah" and "Beautiful Dreamer," and he was an occasional visitor. In 1854, the building was bought by Edward's brother, James Buchanan, the only Pennsylvanian to serve as President. Today, a variety of Continental dishes, from prime rib and porterhouse steak to veal Marsala, lobster tails and chicken chardonnay, are served by crackling fires in two dining rooms with thick stone walls, colonial decor and mellow candlelit atmosphere. *Moderate– expensive. Mon–Sat 5pm–10pm, Sun 4pm–9pm. Bar and wine list. Reservations recommended. All major credit cards.*

Shady Maple Smorgasbord
1352 Main Street, East Earl, PA 17519. Tel: 717-354-8222.

Pace yourself! The all-you-can-eat buffet is piled high with rib-sticking Pennsylvania Dutch specialties. Meat loaf and gravy, roast beef, succulent ham, fluffy mashed potatoes, corn on the cob and other down-home dishes are just a tong's reach away. Baked goods are made daily at the neighboring Shady Maple Farm Market. Be sure to leave room for dessert: make-your-own sundaes, custard, cakes, pies, pudding and more. Eat as much as you like. But remember, doggy bags are forbidden. *Moderate. Breakfast Mon–Sat 5am–10am; lunch Mon–Fri 10:45am–3:15pm; dinner Mon–Fri 4pm–8pm, Sat 10:45am–8pm. Reservations available Mon–Fri; no Sat reservations. Alcohol is not permitted. All major credit cards.*

Stoltzfus Farm
Route 772, Intercourse, PA 17534. Tel: 717-768-8156.

Homemade sausage and ham loaf are among the specialties prepared at the nearby butcher shop and served family-style at this former Amish farmhouse just east of the village. Other Dutch favorites like fried chicken, candied sweet potatoes, buttered noodles, chow chow and peppered cabbage round out the meal, finished with a variety of freshly baked desserts including shoofly pie, cherry crumb and carrot cake. Still hungry? Go ahead and help yourself to seconds. Customers pay one price and eat all they want. *Moderate. Dinner Mon–Sat*

May–Oct 11:30am–8pm, weekends only Apr and Nov. Reservations recommended. MC, V.

What to Do

ATTRACTIONS

Aaron & Jessica's Buggy Rides
Old Philadelphia Pike (Route 340) at Plain & Fancy Farm, Bird-in-Hand, PA 17504. Tel: 717-768-8828.

A guided, 25-minute tour of Amish farms in a traditional horse-drawn buggy. *Mon–Sat 8am–dusk. $10 adults, $5 children (age 3–12).*

Abe's Buggy Rides
2596 Old Philadelphia Pike (Route 340), Bird-in-Hand, PA 17504. Tel: 717-392-1794.

A 25-minute, two-mile narrated ride through Amish country in a horse-drawn carriage. *Mon–Sat Apr–Oct 8am–7pm, Nov–Mar 9am–dusk. $10 adults, $5 children (age 3–12).*

American Military Edged Weaponry Museum
3562 Old Philadelphia Pike (Route 340), Intercourse, PA 17534. Tel: 717-768-7185.

A collection of some 3,000 bayonets, sabers, knives and other military equipment and memorabilia from the Revolutionary War to the present day. *Mon–Sat 10am–5:30pm.*

Amish Experience

3121 Old Philadelphia Pike (Route 340), Bird-in-Hand, PA 17504. Tel: 717-768-8400.

There are three attractions at the Plain & Fancy Farm: The multimedia **Amish Experience F/X Theater** presents *Jacob's Choice*, a fictional tale of an Amish family; the **Amish Country Homestead** is a recreated Amish farmhouse; and **Amish Country Tours** are narrated motorcoach tours tracing the area's history and culture. *F/X Theater Apr–Jun Mon–Sat 9am–5pm, Sun 11am–6pm; Jul–Oct Mon–Sat 9am–8pm, Sun 11am–6pm. $6 adults, $3.50 children (age 4–11). Amish Country Homestead Apr–Jun and Nov Mon–Sat 9:45am–4:30pm, Sun 10:45am–4:45pm; Jul–Oct Mon–Sat 9:45am–6:45pm, Sun 10:45am–4:45pm; call for winter hours. $4.50 adults, $3 children (age 4–11). Amish Country Tours Apr–Oct Mon–Sat 10:30am and 2pm, Sun 11:30am; call for winter hours. $17.95 adults, $10.95 children (age 4–11).*

Amish Farm and House

2395 Lincoln Highway East (Route 30), Lancaster, PA 17602. Tel: 717-394-6185.

A model Amish farm with a 19th-century house and bank barn, windmill, blacksmith shop, livestock and covered bridge. *Daily 8:30am–4pm, extended summer hours. $5.50 adults, $3 children (age 5–11).*

Amish Village

Route 896, Strasburg, PA 17579. Tel: 717-687-8511.

A recreation of an Amish settlement, with an 1840 farmhouse, blacksmith shop, smokehouse and barn. *Summer daily 9am–6pm, spring and fall daily 9am–5pm, winter daily 9am–4pm. $5.50 adults, $1.50 children (age 6–12).*

Dutch Wonderland

2249 Lincoln Highway East (Route 30), Lancaster, PA 17602. Tel: 717-291-1888.

A 44-acre amusement park with all the classic rides – roller coasters, carousel, water slide, monorail and more – as well as a diving show, entertainment and lovely gardens. *Call for hours. $19 adults and children over 5, $14.50 children (age 3–5).*

Folk Craft Center

Mount Sidney Road, Witmer, PA 17585. Tel: 717-397-3609.

Two floors of Pennsylvania Dutch artifacts and antiques as well as an 18th-century herb garden, woodworker's shop, slide show, working 19th-century loom. *Apr–Nov Mon–Sat 10am–5pm, Sun 11am–4pm. $5 adults, $4 seniors, $2.50 children (under 16).*

Mascot Roller Mill

Stumptown Road (at Route 772), Bird-in-Hand, PA 17505.

A free tour details the history and operation of this historic mill, built in 1760 and still used by Amish farmers. *May–Oct Mon–Sat 9am–4pm.*

Mill Bridge Village

South Ronks Road, Strasburg, PA 17579. Tel: 717-687-8181.

A collection of historic buildings and reproductions, including a 1738 gristmill, recreated Amish home, covered bridge, buggy rides and working blacksmith, broom maker, quilters and woodworkers. *Apr–Nov 10am–5pm. $10 adults, $5 children (age 6–12).*

People's Place
3513 Old Philadelphia Pike (Route 340), Intercourse, PA 17534. Tel: 717-768-7171.

A three-screen documentary film, *Who Are the Amish?,* and Amish World museum provide a sensitive and informative portrayal of Amish and Mennonite culture. An excellent bookstore is on the first floor, and the **Old Country Store**, an associated quilt and craft shop, is across the street. *Mon–Sat 9:30am–5pm, extended summer hours. $4 adults, $2 children (age 12 and under).*

U.S. Hot Air Balloon Team
Hopewell Road, P.O. Box 490, St. Peters, PA 19470. Tel: 800-763-5987.

Soar above Amish country in a hot-air balloon. Passengers meet at Rockvale Square; champagne and snacks are served after the flight. *Daily at sunrise and sunset. $89 for 30 minutes, $139 for an hour.*

Wax Museum of Lancaster County History
2249 Lincoln Highway East (Route 30), Lancaster, PA 17602. Tel: 717-393-3679.

A series of wax-figure dioramas chronicles the most important episodes and people in Lancaster history. The exhibit is capped off by a dramatization of an Amish barn-raising. *Daily 9am–5pm (to 8pm in summer). $5.75 adults, $3.25 children (age 5–11).*

Weavertown One-Room Schoolhouse
2249 Lincoln Highway East (Route 30), Lancaster, PA 17602. Tel: 717-768-3976 or 717-291-1888.

A 19th-century one-room schoolhouse occupied by animated figures depicting the activities of a typical Amish school. *Mar and Nov Sat–Sun 10am–5pm, Apr–Oct daily 10am–5pm, extended summer hours. $2.75 adults, $2.25 seniors, $1.75 children (age 5–11).*

ARTS & ENTERTAINMENT

American Music Theatre
2425 Lincoln Highway East (Route 30), Lancaster, PA 17605. Tel: 717-397-7700.

Rousing musical revues and holiday shows are featured at this grand modern theater. *Tue–Sun. $25 adults, $12.50 children (age 3–17).*

Rainbow Dinner Theater
Lincoln Highway East (Route 30), Paradise, PA 17562. Tel: 717-299-4300 or toll-free 800-292-4301.

The theater presents comedies, dramas and musicals while the audience enjoys a full dinner. *Tue–Sun. $30–$34.*

WHITE HORSE -7
INTERCOURSE
FORMERLY "CROSS KEYS"
FROM A NOTED OLD TAVERN STAND
FOUNDED
1754

Redware pottery decorated with a "double distelfink," symbol of good luck and happiness.

SHOPPING

Bird-in-Hand Bake Shop
542 Gibbons Road, Bird-in-Hand, PA 17505. Tel: 717-656-7947.

Shoofly pies, sticky buns, cinnamon rolls, whoopie pies, cakes, breads, cookies and other Dutch sweets are made at this divinely aromatic bakery in the countryside outside town. *Mon–Sat 9am–5pm.*

Bird-in-Hand Farmers' Market
Old Philadelphia Pike (Route 340) and Maple Avenue, Bird-in-Hand, PA 17505. Tel: 717-393-9674.

A lively indoor market with about 30 stalls selling fresh produce, smoked meats and sausage, baked goods, candy, crafts and more. *Fri–Sat 8:30am–5:30pm, Wed Apr–Nov 8:30am–5:30pm, Thu Jul–Oct 8:30am–5:30pm.*

Clay Distelfink
2246 Old Philadelphia Pike (Route 340), Lancaster, PA 17602. Tel: 717-399-1994.

Classic redware pottery carved and painted by hand with traditional Pennsylvania Dutch designs. Custom-made plates are a specialty. *Mon–Sat 9am–5pm.*

Country Knives
4134 Old Philadelphia Pike (Route 340), Intercourse, PA 17534. Tel: 717-768-3818.

From samurai swords to cuticle clippers, this shop carries one of the largest collections of fine cutlery you've ever seen – hunting knives, daggers, culinary knives, cleavers and ornamental blades with beautiful inlaid handles. *Mon–Sat 9am–5:30pm, Sun noon–4:30pm.*

Country Lane Quilts and Woodworking
211 South Groffdale Road, Leola, PA 17540. Tel: 717-656-8476.

Picnic tables, wishing wells and custom-built gazebos as well as dozens of hand-sewn quilts offered at a working farm and workshop. *Mon–Sat dawn–dusk.*

Dutch Barn Antiques
3272 West Newport Road, Ronks, PA 17572. Tel: 717-768-3067.

It may look like a junkyard to the uninitiated, but closer inspection reveals antique plows, iron stoveplates, hay wagons, Amish buggies, ice cream makers, sleds and other barnyard and household items. A real treasure for devoted browsers. *Mon–Sat 9am–6pm.*

Fishercraft Custom-Built Furniture
123 Groffdale Church Road, Leola, PA 17540. Tel: 717-656-8728.

Hardwood tables, chairs, cupboards and hutches are made to your specifications at this workshop and showroom on a traditional Amish farm. *Mon–Fri 7am–5pm, Sat 7am–3pm.*

Fisher's Handmade Quilts

2715 Old Philadelphia Pike (Route 340), Bird-in-Hand, PA 17505. Tel: 717-392-5440.

A popular shop on the second floor of the Bird-in-Hand Bakery, with quilts, wallhangings and pillows produced by Amish and Mennonite craftspeople. *Mon–Sat 9am–5pm.*

Fisher's Quality Furniture

3061 Newport Road (Route 772), Ronks, PA 17572. Tel: 717-656-4423.

Oak and cherry furniture in a variety of early-American styles is handcrafted at this Amish farm and workshop. The quality is high and the prices reasonable. *Mon–Fri 8am–5pm, Sat 9:30am–3:30pm.*

Hayloft Candles

South Groffdale Road, Leola, PA 17540.

Enjoy homemade ice cream while browsing among scores of fragrant candles and an assortment of other crafts, books and household items. Kids will get a kick out of the goats, ducks and few exotic animals in a little barnyard zoo next to the store. *Mon–Sat 9am–6pm, Fri 9am–8pm.*

Intercourse Canning Company

3612 East Newport Road, Intercourse, PA 17534. Tel: 717-768-0156.

Chow chow, pepper relish, pumpkin butter, corn salsa, jams, dressings and other Dutch favorites are canned before your eyes by Amish and Mennonite people and sold at this cavernous old building in the center of town. Free samples and shipping are available. *Apr–Dec Mon–Sat 9am–5pm, Jan–Mar Mon–Sat 10am–5pm.*

Intercourse Pretzel Factory

Cross Keys Village Center, 3614 Old Philadelphia Pike (Route 340), Intercourse, PA 17534. Tel: 717-768-3432.

Tour the plant, try your hand at pretzel twisting, and enjoy a taste of the finished product – traditional soft and hard pretzels as well as a few specialty items like chocolate-covered pretzels and pretzels stuffed with sausage, bologna or cream cheese and jelly. *Mon–Sat 9am–6pm; factory tour Tue–Sat 9am–4pm; call for extended summer hours.*

Kauffman's Handcrafted Clocks

3019 West Newport Road (Route 772), Ronks, PA 17572. Tel: 717-656-6857.

A collection of handsome clocks – grandfather, grandmother, mantle, cuckoo, banjo, even pocket watches – handcrafted from walnut, cherry or oak with precision German movements. Customers can buy from stock or have a clock custom-built. *Mon–Fri 9am–5pm, Sat 9am–4pm.*

Kauffman's Hardware

201–15 East Main Street (Route 23), New Holland, PA 17557. Tel: 717-354-4606.

Looking for an antique bed pan? An old-fashioned water pump? A potbellied stove? Amish cigars? You'll find these and hundreds of other rustic wares at this historic country store, open since 1779. The old brick building also served as a post office, town hall, jail and fire company.

Mon 6:30am–8pm, Tue–Wed 6:30am–5:30pm, Thu 6:30am–8pm, Fri 6:30am–9pm, Sat 6:30am–5pm.

Kitchen Kettle Village
Old Philadelphia Pike (Route 340), Intercourse, PA 17534.
Tel: 717-768-8261 or toll-free 800-732-3538.

Thirty-two specialty shops in a "country village" centered around the Kitchen Kettle jam and relish kitchen. Inquire about special events, including the Rhubarb Festival in May, the Gathering of Local Arts and Artists in July, and the Seven Sweets and Seven Sours Festival in September. *Mon–Fri 9am–5pm, Sat 9am–5:30pm.*

Lapp's Coach Shop
3572 West Newport Road (Route 772), Intercourse, PA 17534.
Tel: 717-768-8712.

Just across from Kitchen Kettle Village, this shop sells a variety of pine and oak furniture, cedar chests, bentwood rockers, birdhouses, mailboxes and rocking horses. It's probably best-known, however, for the dozens of little red wagons that are parked in the front lot. Most items are made by Amish crafts-men. *Summer Mon–Sat 8am–6pm, winter Mon–Sat 8am–5pm.*

Lapp Valley Farm Homemade Ice Cream
244 Mentzer Road, New Holland, PA 17557.

Ice cream doesn't get any fresher than this stuff, made on the Lapp family's 60-acre dairy farm and sold at a little shop next to the house. It's also available at Kitchen Kettle Village in Inter-course and the Green Dragon Farmers' Market in Ephrata. *Mon–Thu 10am–7pm, Fri–Sat 8am–7pm.*

Handmade crafts, toys and furniture are available in shops throughout Amish country.

Little Book Shop
2710 Old Philadelphia Pike (Route 340), Bird-in-Hand, PA 17505. Tel: 717-295-7580.

The name says it all: a petite bookstore next to the Bird-in-Hand Farmers' Market with a selection of new and used books, mostly paperbacks. *Call for hours.*

Meadowbrook Farmers' Market
Route 23, Leola, PA 17540. Tel: 717-656-2226.

A sprawling country market with an assortment of fresh produce, meats and baked goods as well as antiques, gifts and housewares. *Fri 9am–8pm, Sat 8am–5pm.*

Old Candle Barn
Old Philadelphia Pike (Route 340), Intercourse, PA 17534. Tel: 717-768-8926.

A cavernous place next to Kitchen Kettle Village filled with every sort of candle and other crafts and gifts. *Mon–Sat 10am–5:30pm.*

Old Village Store
Old Philadelphia Pike (Route 340), Bird-in-Hand, PA 17505. Tel: 717-397-1291.

Founded in 1890, this rambling old hardware store is now mostly devoted to the tourist trade, with a wide variety of country housewares, gifts and souvenirs, and an indoor "kissing bridge." *Mon–Sat 9am–5pm, extended hours in summer.*

Rockvale Square Outlets
Routes 30 and 896, Lancaster, PA 17602. Tel: 717-293-9595.

You'll find discounts on everything from the fanciful to the utilitarian at more than 100 outlets, including well-known brand names like the Gap, Anne Klein, Levi's, Laura Ashley, Black & Decker, Sony and Nike. *Mar–Dec Mon–Sat 9:30am–9pm, Sun noon–6pm; Jan–Feb Mon–Thu 9:30am–6pm, Fri–Sat 9:30am–9pm, Sun noon–6pm.*

Rohrer's Mill
273 Rohrer Mill Road, Ronks, PA 17572. Tel: 717-687-6400.

Stone-ground whole wheat flour, roasted corn meal, oatmeal, buckwheat and other all-natural, homegrown grains are sold directly to the public at this traditional water-powered mill, built in 1852 and run by the same family for more than 75 years. *Mon–Sat 7:30am–5pm.*

Smucker's Quilts
117 North Groffdale Road, New Holland, PA 17557. Tel: 717-656-8730.

Set on a family farm, this basement shop has scores of heirloom-quality quilts sewn by local Plain women. Shams, pillows, wall hangings and pot holders are also available. *Mon–Sat 8am–8pm.*

Tanger Factory Outlet Center
Route 30 East, Lancaster, PA 17602. Tel: 717-392-7260 or toll-free 800-408-3477.

More than 50 factory outlets with clothing, home furnishings, footwear, exercise equipment and more. *Mon–Sat 9:30am–9pm, Sun 11am–6pm.*

Thomas B. Morton Cabinetmakers
30 South Hershey Avenue, Leola, PA 17540. Tel: 717-656-3799.

Morton takes a contemporary approach to traditional furniture design, emphasizing clean lines, masterful joinery, and high quality wood, usually cherry. Customers can choose from stock designs or have something custom-made. Remodeling and period reproductions are also available. The work isn't cheap, but considering the high level of quality it's fairly priced. Morton also has a display at the Artworks at Doneckers. *Tue–Fri 9am–5pm.*

Will-Char, The Hex Place
3056 Lincoln Highway East (Route 30), Paradise, PA 17562. Tel: 717-687-8329.

The shop carries a variety of gifts and souvenirs but specializes in Pennsylvania German hex signs, "good omens" that are traditionally painted on barns and houses. *Mon–Sat 9am–6pm, Sun 9am–5pm.*

Witmer Quilt Shop
1070–76 West Main Street, New Holland, PA 17557. Tel: 717-656-9526.

In business for more than 35 years, this little shop is piled high with more than 150 expertly crafted quilts in a wide variety of colors and patterns, many designed by owner Emma Witmer. *Mon 8am–8pm, Tue– Thu 8am–6pm, Fri 8am–8pm, Sat 8am–6pm.*

W.L. Zimmerman & Sons
3601 Old Philadelphia Pike (Route 340), Intercourse, PA 17534. Tel: 717-768-8291.

An old-fashioned country store with groceries, hardware and a large Amish clientele. *Mon–Sat 7am–9pm.*

OUTDOOR RECREATION

Lancaster Host Resort
2300 Lincoln Highway (Route 30), Lancaster, PA 17602. Tel: 717-299-5500.

A full-service resort with 27 holes of golf, tennis courts, pools, restaurants and more.

SPECIAL EVENTS

March
Gordonville Fire Company Auction
Old Leacock Road, Gordonville, PA 17529. Tel: 717-768-3869.

This lively sale of farm equipment, livestock, antiques and other items is heavily attended by the Amish and offers a fascinating glimpse into community life.

April
Annual Quilters' Heritage Celebration
Holiday Inn Lancaster Host Hotel, 2300 Lincoln Highway (Route 30), Lancaster, PA 17602. Tel: 717-299-5500.

Demonstrations, gatherings and sales featuring some of the area's best quilters.

May
A Gathering of Local Art & Artists Rhubarb Festival
Kitchen Kettle Village, Old Philadelphia Pike (Route 340), Intercourse, PA 17534. Tel: 717-768-8261 or toll-free 800-732-3538.

Two events welcome spring at Kitchen Kettle Village. The first is a celebration of quilting, tinsmithing, pottery and other traditional crafts. The other is a festival with homecooked food, live music and lots of rhubarb.

An Amish buggy passes through Hunsecker's Mill Bridge, near Eden.

June
Route 340 Food & Folk Fair
Old Philadelphia Pike (Route 340),
Bird-in-Hand, PA 17505.
Tel: 717-768-8272.

An open-air festival showcasing some of the finest restaurants and craftsmen in the area.

September
Seven Sweets and Sours Festival
Kitchen Kettle Village,
Old Philadelphia Pike (Route 340),
Intercourse, PA 17534.
Tel: 717-768-8261 or toll-free 800-732-3538.

A harvest festival with tastings of chow chow, corn salsa and other Dutch specialties.

Gordonville Fire Company Auction
Old Leacock Road, Gordonville,
PA 17529. Tel: 717-768-3869.

A great opportunity to mingle with the community at a high-energy sale of livestock, buggies, quilts and other farm-related items.

INFORMATION

Mennonite Information Center
2209 Millstream Road, Lancaster,
PA 17602-1494. Tel: 717-299-0954.

The center offers a variety of services and information – exhibits on Amish and Mennonite culture, books, postcards, a Mennonite step-on guide service, a reproduction of the Hebrew Tabernacle, and free maps, brochures and a movie.
Mon–Sat 8am–5pm.

Pennsylvania Dutch Convention and Visitors Bureau
501 Greenfield Road, Lancaster,
PA 17601. Tel: 717-299-8901 or toll-free 800-723-8824.

Mon–Sat 8am–6pm, Sun 8am–5pm.

HIGHLIGHTS

- Central Market
- Heritage Center Museum
- Wheatland
- Rock Ford Plantation
- Landis Valley Museum

Lancaster

Courtyards, winding alleys, historic brick town houses – they give charm to this handsome city set in the heart of Pennsylvania Dutch Country.

Lancaster was known as Hickory Town before being laid out as a city in 1730 by Andrew Hamilton. It quickly became the largest inland settlement in the colonies and a major portal to the frontier.

Nowadays there's an interesting cast of characters: Amish and Mennonite farmers bringing their goods to market; art students sipping latte at one of several hip cafes; professional couples enjoying dinner at a smart downtown bistro; and a relatively new community of Hispanic immigrants.

In early times, trade with Indians was brisk, and in 1744 their leaders throughout the region gathered at Lancaster to swear allegiance to the English in their war with the French. Relations took a dark turn about 20 years later, however, when a band of vigilantes known as the Paxton Boys raided a peaceful band of Conestoga Indians and killed all they could find. The survivors took refuge in the

The Central Market in Lancaster is the oldest operating farmers' market in the country. Above, architectural detail at the Southern Market building.

Lancaster jail, only to be slaughtered there a few months later by the Paxtons.

The American Revolution left Lancaster relatively unscathed. The Continental Congress took refuge here when the British occupied Philadelphia in 1777, and for one day Lancaster served as the nation's capital. It was also twice the state capital, first in 1777–78 and again from 1799 to 1812.

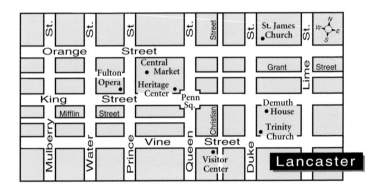

The best way to explore all of Lancaster's historic nooks and crannies is on foot. Start at the town center, **Penn Square**, where the **Soldiers and Sailors Monument**, erected in 1874, honors the men who fell during the Civil War. Just around the corner is **Central Market**, the nation's oldest continuously operating farmers' market, now listed on the National Register of Historic Places. The Romanesque Revival structure was built in 1889, but a market had existed here at least 150 years earlier. In fact, Andrew Hamilton, the founder of Lancaster, deeded land at this spot for "keeping, erecting and holding a market" in 1730. It was said that "no fruit, vegetable or cereal cultivated anywhere in the state was lacking" here, and it remains true. In addition to fruits and vegetables, you'll find regional specialties like Lancaster sausage, scrapple and sweet bologna, and cholesterol-soaked goodies like shoofly and whoopie pie. You'll have to wake up early to catch the "plain folk" carting their goods to town; they usually arrive well before sunrise.

Just a few steps away on the northwest corner of Penn Square is **Old City Hall**, one of Lancaster's few public buildings dating to the late 18th century. Pennsylvania government occupied the building for several years in the early 1800s during the city's second stint as the capital. Today the building serves as the **Heritage Center of Lancaster County**, featuring an impressive collection of quilts, weather vanes, rifles, pottery and other folk art produced during the early days of settlement. An adjacent shop carries a variety of traditional arts and crafts.

It's a quick two-block walk from the Heritage Center to the **Fulton Opera House**, one of the country's oldest theaters still in operation. Built in 1852 (at the site of the jail where the Paxton Boys attacked the Conestoga Indians) and listed in the National Register of Historic Places, the four-story opera house was considered one of the finest and largest venues of its kind in Pennsylvania. Apparently early patrons didn't mind the smoke and powder

Named for inventor Robert Fulton, a Lancaster County native, the Fulton Opera House has been a center of the performing arts for more than a century.

drifting down from a fourth-floor shooting gallery or the stench of fertilizer and tobacco stored in the basement.

Many luminaries have appeared here over the years. Mark Twain lectured in 1872. Buffalo Bill Cody and Wild Bill Hickok staged their melodramatic *Scouts of the Plains* in 1873. W.C. Fields did his wisecracking routine in 1907. Today, the Fulton presents a variety of cultural events – opera, symphonic music, children's theater – as well as a well-regarded series of Broadway shows, musicals and new drama.

Return to Penn Square and turn right on Queen Street. It's about half a block to the **Lancaster Newspaper Newseum**, a sidewalk exhibit that chronicles the development of newspapers over the centuries. Nearby, at 100 South Queen Street, is the **Southern Market Downtown Visitors Center**. Once the site of a farmers' market, the building now houses the **Lancaster Chamber of Commerce** and **Historic Lancaster Walking Tour** – a daily 90-minute jaunt led by a costumed guide to the most historic places in the downtown area.

Return again to Penn Square and turn right on King Street, where you'll find an interesting collection of local memorabilia at the **Demuth Tobacco Shop**, said to be the oldest in the United States; it's been operated by the same family since 1770. The modest 18th-century town house next door is the former residence of **Charles Demuth**, one of the country's most distinguished

One of the country's most distinguished watercolorists, Demuth produced more than a thousand works, many in his studio on King Street.

watercolorists. Although plagued by illness much of his life, Demuth – or "Deem" as his friends called him – produced more than a thousand works, many of them in a snug second-floor studio overlooking the garden. He was particularly noted for incorporating the geometric shapes of machinery and equipment. His well-known *My Egypt,* for example, was inspired by the grain elevators in the countryside around the city. Demuth died in Lancaster in 1935. The house and garden are open to visitors; a gallery features his work.

Don't miss the historic churches in the area. The stately brick mass of **Trinity Lutheran Church,** just around the corner at 31 South Duke Street, is among the most impressive. It was established in 1766 and houses one of the city's oldest congregations. About two blocks north, at East Orange and North Duke streets, is **St. James Episcopal Church,** built in 1744. Several prominent people are buried in the churchyard, including George Ross, a signer of the Declaration of Independence, and Gen. Edward Hand, who served as George Washington's adjutant-general during the Revolution. A long row of slabs near the rear of the church belongs to the Coleman family. Robert Coleman, a delegate to the Constitutional Convention, was one of the wealthiest ironmasters in Pennsylvania. His daughter Anne was engaged to James Buchanan, but her father didn't think much of the young lawyer, and the nuptials never took place. She died soon after, apparently brokenhearted, and Buchanan later became the only bachelor President to occupy the White House.

Trinity Lutheran Church, one of several historic churches in downtown Lancaster.

Just beyond downtown, in the northwest corner of the city, you can stroll past the noble Gothic buildings and century-old shade trees of **Franklin and Marshall College**, or browse the neighboring **North Museum of Natural History and Science**, which has everything from Egyptian artifacts and dinosaur bones to a high-tech planetarium.

A short drive west of downtown is **Wheatland**, at 1120 Marietta Ave., home of James Buchanan from 1848 until his death in 1868. Buchanan regarded the mansion – a handsome Federal structure built in 1828 and furnished with many of his personal belongings – as a "beau ideal of a statesman's abode." It was here that he found refuge from "the troubles, perplexities, and difficulties" of public life. As President, his equivocation on the issue of slavery inflamed extremists in both North and South and did little to stop the nation's slide toward Civil War. An informative 45-minute tour outlines Buchanan's life and career; highlights include the desk where the President-elect composed his inaugural address; a portrait of Anne Coleman, his disappointed fiancée; and a grand piano belonging to his orphaned niece, Harriet Lane, who lived with Buchanan at Wheatland and accompanied him to the White House.

On the banks of the Conestoga River about a mile south of town is **Rock Ford Plantation** (881 Rock Ford Road), a beautifully preserved 1792 Georgian manor once occupied by Gen. Edward Hand. Trained as a physician in Ireland, Hand served alongside George Washington during the Revolution and was later elected to the Pennsylvania Assembly and U.S. Congress. Among the many personal items in the house are an unusual long-

> **By 1775, Lancaster was the largest inland city in the colonies and a major portal to the frontier.**

backed chair made especially for the general, who stood well over six feet tall, as well as a portable field desk with secret compartments that he used during the war. A barn on the property houses the **Kauffman Museum**, a collection of 18th- and 19th-century handicrafts and decorative arts, with hundreds of samples of stoneware, pewter, copper, long rifles and fraktur, a form of illuminated writing.

Two other museums on the outskirts of town are well worth a side trip, too. The **Landis Valley Museum**, 2451 Kissel Hill Road, illustrates the rural life-style of Pennsylvania Germans in the 19th century. Visitors are invited to explore an entire village of historic buildings, including farmsteads, a tavern, country store, harness shop and firehouse filled with thousands of tools, household objects and farm equipment. Demonstrations of various crafts and occupations such as weaving, potting and tinsmithing are held in summer and fall.

If you're traveling with kids, don't pass up the nearby **Hands-On House Children's Museum** at 2380 Kissel Hill Road. The entire place is dedicated to the fine art of child's play. Eight interactive exhibits, including face painting, an assembly line, and a fantasy forest, are designed for youngsters ranging in age from two to 10.

The stately neoclassical facade of the Old County Courthouse.

Where to Stay

Apple Bin Inn

2835 Willow Street Pike, Willow Street, PA 17584. Tel: 717-464-5881 or toll-free 800-338-4296. Fax: 717-464-1818.

Built in 1865, this former general store sits close to the main road in the little town of Willow Street about four miles from downtown Lancaster. Common rooms include a comfortable living room with a combination of colonial antiques and reproductions and an old piano. A full breakfast of, say, German apple pancakes, quiche or French toast with warm caramel pecan sauce is served at two tables in the dining room or, if weather permits, on the back patio. There are three bedrooms on the second floor, two with a separate sitting room. Another is in the carriage house, which has a private living room, a gas fireplace and snug second-story bedroom. All rooms are furnished in country style with a variety of quilts, comforters, hook rugs, four-poster beds and other Shaker and Amish touches. *Rates: $95–$135 double occupancy; two-night minimum on weekends July–November and holidays. Children over 12 are welcome; no pets. Amenities: Five rooms with private bath (one is in the corridor), cable television and air conditioning, including two-room suites and a two-story carriage house with gas fireplace. Fax machine, patio, parking. AE, MC, V.*

☆ Gardens of Eden

1894 Eden Road, Lancaster, PA 17601. Tel: 717-393-5179. Fax: 717-393-7722.

Built about 1867 by a local iron-master, this early Victorian, red-brick house is an oasis of country charm just 10 minutes from downtown Lancaster. Perched on 3 1/2 meticulously tended acres overlooking the Conestoga River and surrounded by a bounty of ferns, flowers and blossoming trees, the inn offers three rooms and a cottage artfully decorated with family heirlooms, folk art, hanging quilts and antique furnishings. Abundant arrangements of dried and fresh flowers are the handiwork of innkeeper Marilyn Ebel, a floral designer, who keeps a studio and gift shop in the original stone kitchen. The two largest rooms in the main house have a view of the river and are tastefully furnished with king- or queen-sized mahogany beds, antique rocker, Chippendale dresser, oriental rugs, wide-plank floors and other charming touches. The snug, two-story cottage features a walk-in fireplace and kitchenette with tin panel cupboards; a narrow staircase winds to a small bedroom tucked under the eaves. Common areas include a living room with fireplace, wood floors, a baby-grand piano and comfy sofas. A full breakfast of fresh fruit, muesli, baked goods and perhaps an egg dish, waffles or French toast is often prepared with homegrown herbs and edible flowers, one of Marilyn's specialties. Breakfast is served at a single table in the dining room or in a lovely screened porch that opens to a flagstone patio in the back garden. Personal tours and dinner with an Amish family can be arranged with advance notice. *Rates: $85–$130 double occupancy; two-night minimum on weekends, three-night minimum on holidays. Children are welcome in the cottage; no pets. Amenities: four rooms with private bath and air conditioning; fireplace, telephone and cable television in the cottage. Extensive gardens, patio, canoeing, fishing, parking. MC, V.*

Hotel Brunswick
Chestnut and Queen Streets, Lancaster, PA 17608.
Tel: 717-397-4801 or toll-free 800-233-0182.

This nine-story downtown hotel offers a wide range of amenities and is popular with business people and families. Standard rooms have a king- or two queen-sized beds; many have been recently renovated. *Rates: $54–$86 double occupancy. Wheelchair-accessible; children under 17 stay free in the same room as adults; cribs free; small pets are welcome with advance notice. Amenities: 224 rooms with private bath, air conditioning, cable television, telephone. Restaurant, nightclub with live entertainment, banquet and conference facilities, indoor pool, fitness center, room service, gift shop, parking. Ask about package deals and other discounts. All major credit cards.*

★ King's Cottage
1049 East King Street, Lancaster, PA 17602. Tel: 717-397-1017 or toll-free 800-747-8717. Fax: 717-397-3447.

Set on a busy road about five minutes from downtown Lancaster, this spacious, well-appointed house was built in 1913 by a dentist and transformed in the mid-1980s into a bed-and-breakfast. It's now listed in the National Register of Historic Places, owing largely to its unusual blend of architecture, including a distinct Spanish Mission exterior. The interior includes an airy living room and library with glossy wood floors, marble fireplaces and elegant furnishings, and a large solarium that opens to a clay-tile patio. A full breakfast is served at a large table in the formal dining room and may include entrees like stuffed French toast, quiche, frittatas or ham-and-cheese crepes with Hollandaise sauce. Guest rooms are furnished with antique armoires and dressers, armchairs, settees and queen- or king-sized beds, some with hand-carved headboards or canopies. You'll find an extra measure of privacy in the carriage house, which features a fireplace and two-person Jacuzzi, or in the first-floor bedroom, which has a private outside entrance. Two cozy rooms on the third floor are somewhat smaller and have low ceilings but are pretty nonetheless. *Rates: $100–$175 double occupancy; two-night minimum on weekends, three-night minimum on holidays. The carriage house is wheelchair-accessible; children over 12 are welcome; no pets. Amenities: nine rooms with private bath (three are in the corridor) and air conditioning; carriage house with fireplace and Jacuzzi; telephone and television on request; patio, water garden, parking. DC, Dis, MC, V.*

★ indicates a personal favorite of the author

☆ **Maison Rouge**
2236 Marietta Avenue,
P.O. Box 6243, Lancaster, PA 17601.
Tel: 717-399-3033 or toll-free
800-309-3033.

Set on a busy street of homes and businesses about three miles from downtown is this large and stately Victorian mansion with a wraparound veranda and slate mansard roof. Built in the Second Empire style in 1882 by state senator John Stehman and used for many years as a doctor's office, the house has been fully renovated to reflect the formal charm of the era. The foyer is flanked on either side by twin parlors with high ceilings, hardwood floors, a crystal chandelier and original woodwork. Both are furnished with a collection of straight-backed chairs, settees and other period antiques. A full breakfast is served at a single large table set with silver, china and crystal in a formal dining room, and may include entrees like eggs Benedict or stuffed French toast. An impressive winding staircase leads to four second-story bedrooms tastefully furnished with lace curtains and drapes, antiques and oriental rugs. Some rooms have a four-poster bed or ornate carved headboard, and there's one with a particularly impressive Chippendale canopy bed. A lovely garden in the backyard is perfect for early-morning coffee or a late-night aperitif. *Rates: $95– $125 double occupancy; two-night minimum on holidays and select weekends. Children over 12 are welcome; no pets. Amenities: four bedrooms with private bath (one is in the corridor) and air conditioning. Garden, patio, parking. AE, MC, V.*

Willow Valley Family Resort
2416 Willow Street Pike
(Route 222), Lancaster, PA 17602.
Tel: 717-464-2711 or toll-free
800-444-1714. Fax: 717-464-4784.

Situated about 15 minutes from downtown Lancaster, this attractive, family-oriented resort offers comfortable hotel accommodations and a host of facilities, including a nine-hole golf course, lighted tennis courts, indoor and outdoor pools, and a popular smorgasbord restaurant. Standard rooms are furnished with two queen- or one king-sized bed; two-room suites are available with pullout sofa, some with Jacuzzi and/or balcony. An abundant Sunday brunch is served in the Palm Court, a dramatic four-story atrium in the main building. A complimentary bus tour of Amish country is offered daily except Sunday. *Rates: $50–$145 double occupancy; two-night minimum on weekends, three-night minimum on holidays. Children are welcome; wheelchair-accessible; no pets. Amenities: 352 rooms with private bath, air conditioning, telephone and cable television. Two indoor and one outdoor pool, sauna, whirlpool, golf course, tennis courts, basketball court, fitness room, game room. Two restaurants, conference and banquet facilities, wedding chapel, bakery, gift shops. Free bus tour Mon–Sat. Garden, patio, parking. All major credit cards.*

Witmer's Tavern
2014 Old Philadelphia Pike
(Route 340), Lancaster, PA 17602.
Tel: 717-299-5305.

Described as Pennsylvania's "most intact and authentic 18th-century inn," this venerable

The Heritage Center Museum is housed in Old City Hall, built in 1795 and listed in the National Register of Historic Places.

stone structure is the last of some 60 taverns that once stood on the old Philadelphia-to-Lancaster Road. Although not the place for luxury lodging, the inn has a quirky, ramshackle charm that some history-minded travelers find delightful. Much of the first floor is taken up by an antique and quilt shop that spills out into a sitting room with everything from museum-quality textiles and period furniture to a scattering of old magazines, prints, books and models. Displays in the entry-way are filled with shards of glass and pottery, rusty nails and an assortment of maps, documents and other household stuff recovered from the days of Conestoga wagons and Indian attacks. Guest rooms are furnished with antiques, including

59

a few with rope beds and feather mattresses. Worn wood floors, exposed brick, thick plaster and original hardware enhance the rustic atmosphere. Most have a fireplace or wood-burning stove; only the two bedrooms on the third floor have private baths. Continental breakfast is included with the room fee. *Rates: $60–$90 double occupancy; $20 extra for use of fireplace. Children over 12 are welcome; no pets. Amenities: seven bedrooms with air conditioning; two rooms with private bath. Antique shop, artifact display, parking. No credit cards.*

Where to Eat

Cafe Angst
114 West Orange Street, Lancaster, PA 17603. Tel: 717-396-1250.

An artsy little place to satisfy your craving for coffee, whether it's freshly brewed espresso, cappuccino or plain old joe. Light fare includes ice cream, muffins, cookies and other baked goods. A full schedule of live music, poetry readings and other happenings make it a hip late-night hangout. *Budget. Sun–Thu 4pm–midnight, Fri–Sat 4pm–3am. No credit cards.*

Caribbean Breeze
219 West King Street, Lancaster, PA 17603. Tel: 717-295-7008.

Had your fill of smorgasbord? Try this funky little place a couple of blocks from Penn Square. Caribbean dishes like jerk chicken, oxtail, curried vegetables and a variety of high-octane tropical drinks are the specialties here. Reggae bands perform on weekend nights; a reggae-stocked jukebox suffices on weekdays. The owners once flew in a limbo instructor from Montego Bay to keep the crowd moving on a Jamaican holiday. *Moderate. Mon–Sat 9am–9pm. Bar. No credit cards.*

D&S Brasserie
1679 Lincoln Highway East (Route 30), Lancaster, PA 17602. Tel: 717-299-1694.

The menu at this friendly meeting place lists a wide variety of familiar dishes, starting with deli sandwiches, burgers and a rich tomato bisque and then moving on to fancier dishes like lemon tarragon chicken, smoked salmon and snow pea Alfredo, prime rib, and pasta. Five dining rooms and a large outdoor deck accommodate everything from family gatherings and business lunches to quiet dinners-for-two. A lively bar with a large-screen television is a good spot for chitchat and finger foods. A solid choice when you need to please a variety of palates at a reasonable price. *Moderate. Lunch Mon–Fri 11:30am–2pm; dinner Sun–Thu 5pm–10pm, Fri–Sat 5pm–11pm. Bar and wine list. Reservations recommended. All major credit cards.*

Gallo Rosso
337–339 North Queen Street,
Lancaster, PA 17603.
Tel: 717-392-5616.

This snazzy trattoria adds an imaginative, contemporary twist to traditional Italian fare. Wines from Italy and California pair well with a variety of pasta dishes like spinach noodles with lamb, eggplant, goat cheese and veal demiglaze, and triangoli stuffed with wild mushrooms and served with spicy sausage. Grilled swordfish and veal portobello are winners, too. Light eaters can stick with antipasto, bruschetta or savory grilled pizza. The energy level is high and increases as the night rolls on. *Moderate. Mon 4:30pm–10pm, Tue–Thu 11:30am–10pm, Fri 11:30am–11pm, Sat 5:30pm–11pm. Bar and wine list. Reservations recommended. All major credit cards.*

Jethro's
First and Ruby Streets, Lancaster,
PA 17603. Tel: 717-299-1700.

The casual appearance of this small neighborhood eatery belies the fine cooking you'll find inside. The small wood-paneled dining room seats about 30 and features artfully prepared dishes like roast pork tenderloin with honey, thyme and garlic, sauteed duck with plum sauce, grilled lamb chops with Arizona chili butter, and a terrific filet mignon. On the lighter side is Cajun shepherd's pie, salmon and black bean burritos, vegetable stirfry, and gourmet pizza. All desserts are homemade; "death by chocolate" is particularly tempting. The work of local artists hangs in the dining room. The low-key bar is decorated with photos of Franklin and Marshall alumni. *Moderate. Mon–Thu 5:30pm–10pm, Fri–Sat 5:30pm–10:30pm. Bar and wine list. Reservations recommended. AE, MC, V.*

★ **J–M's Bistro & Pub**
300 West James Street, Lancaster,
PA 17603. Tel: 717-392-5656.

Master Chef Jean-Maurice Jugé's mission is to serve customers "really, really, really good food." He succeeds. The atmosphere is warm but refined, and the cuisine is filled with a creative mix of ingredients. The menu changes often, but you might start with something intriguing like tequila-cured salmon gravlax or rabbit pâté with sun-dried plums and Armagnac. A few notable entrees include rosemary-scented rack of lamb, crispy seared salmon and a variety of old favorites like Cajun meat loaf, champagne scallop soup, lump crab cakes and tasty 12-inch pizzas. Jugé shares a few culinary secrets at his "Lunch and Learn" cooking classes. Live jazz occasionally spices up the evening. *Moderate–expensive. Mon–Sat 11am–10pm, Sun 11am–9pm. Bar and wine list. Reservations recommended. AE, DC, MC, V.*

Kegel's
551 West King Street, Lancaster,
PA 17603. Tel: 717-397-2832.

Kegel's has been serving fine seafood for more than 50 years. The formula is pretty straightforward: fresh ingredients, simple preparations, and a traditional, family atmosphere. Menu highlights include soft-shell crabs, lobster, crab cakes, and a variety of broiled fish. The catch of the day may have been hooked by one of the owners himself. Meat-eaters won't be disappointed. Kegel's has a reputation for good steaks, too. *Moderate. Tue–Fri 11am–9pm, Sat 2pm–9:30pm, Sun noon–7pm. Bar and wine list. Reservations recommended. AE, Dis, MC, V.*

Lancaster Dispensing Company
33 North Market Street, Lancaster, PA. Tel: 717-299-4602.

Tucked into a brick-paved alley next to the Central Market, this popular watering hole mixes splendid Victorian decor with a relaxed, modern attitude. The menu is dominated by light bites – sandwiches, burgers, salads, finger food and a few vegetarian dishes – complemented by an interesting lineup of beers, including quite a few microbrews. The place draws an animated crowd, especially on Friday and Saturday night. Weekdays tend to be quieter. Live rock, folk and blues are often presented on Thursday, Friday and Saturday night. *Budget–moderate. Mon–Sat 11am–2am, Sun 1pm–10pm. Bar. Reservations accepted. AE, MC, V.*

Lancaster Malt Brewing Company
Plum and Walnut Streets, Lancaster, PA 17602. Tel: 717-391-6258.

Even the most jaded beer drinkers will be delighted by this popular microbrewery, set in an airy, 19th-century warehouse on the east end of town. Exposed beams, wooden stools and shiny brass tabletops add a laid-back, rustic atmosphere, and massive stainless-steel tanks remind beer-lovers why they came. The brew masters are always cooking up something new – golden lager, milk stout, amber ale and specials like maple cranberry and strawberry wheat ales. Intrepid imbibers can choose from several beer mixes like the Plum Street porter float (with vanilla ice cream), shandy (lager and lemonade), roddlermas (lager and ginger ale) and oyster shooter (raw oyster, Tabasco sauce and porter). Dinner entrees are available, but you may be happier with wings, nachos and other pub food and a few house specialties like beer cheese fondue and beer cheese soup. Tours of the brewery are offered daily. *Moderate. Mon–Thu 11:30am–11pm, Fri–Sat 11:30am–1am, Sun 11:30am–10:30pm. Brewery tours daily Mon–Sat 10am–5pm. Reservations accepted. All major credit cards.*

Lanvina Vietnamese
1651 Lincoln Highway East (Route 30), Lancaster, PA 17602. Tel: 717-399-0199.

1762 Columbia Avenue, Lancaster, PA 17603. Tel: 717-393-7748.

Awarded an "excellent" rating by *The World Guide to Vegetarianism,* this casual place in a strip mall just east of town has become well-known among fans of healthful eating. You'll find more than 60 vegetarian delicacies. A few of the more unusual include mock duck in curry sauce, cream cheese wontons, and spicy bean curd with lemon grass. Traditional fare like vegetable lo mein is offered for the less adventurous. Carnivores will find dozens of meat dishes, too. A good choice for an inexpensive, tasty meal. *Budget–*

moderate. Mon–Thu 11am–2pm, dinner 4:30pm–8:30pm; Fri–Sat 11am–9pm. BYOB. MC, V.

The Loft
201 West Orange Street, Lancaster, PA 17602. Tel: 717-299-0661.

This second-story downtown eatery offers convivial lunches and candlelit dinners in an informal setting with a few rustic touches. The menu covers a fairly wide range of American and Continental cuisine: herb-crusted rack of lamb, veal Oscar, roast duck with raspberry tamarind glaze and a variety of steaks, as well as a few simpler choices like salads and burgers for lunch. Appetizers include savory mushroom soup, clams on the half shell and escargot. Watching your diet? Ask for calorie-conscious preparations without butter, salt or sauces, served with steamed vegetables. *Moderate–Expensive. Lunch Mon–Fri 11:30am–2pm; dinner Mon–Sat 5:30pm–10pm. Bar and wine list. Reservations recommended. AE, MC, V.*

Marion Court Room
7 Marion Court, Lancaster, PA 17603. Tel: 717-399-1970.

The atmosphere is warm and relaxing at this casual, gourmet eatery. Diners have a choice of four settings: a traditional dining room, a chatty bar area, an outdoor patio, and an enclosed deck illuminated by strands of twinkly lights. The menu ranges over quite a lot of culinary ground. A few highlights include chicken pesto, rosemary veal, smoked duck fusili and smoked salmon linguine. There are lighter selections, too, including burgers, salads, sandwiches, fancy pizzas and delectable homemade soups. Set in an alley near the courthouse, it's a little tricky to find but worth the search. *Moderate. Lunch Mon–Fri 11am–5pm; dinner daily 5pm–11pm. Bar and wine list. Reservations recommended. AE, Dis, MC, V.*

☆ Market Fare
Grant and Market Streets, Lancaster, PA 17603. Tel: 717-299-7090.

You'll find sophistication without a hint of stuffiness at this popular restaurant, set in the lower level of the former Hager Department Store across from the Central Market. Soothing jazz, 19th-century art, comfy chairs and walls the color of sage and terracotta set the stage for poached salmon with crab and dill sauce, double-cut lamb chops, blackened New York strip steak, grilled beef tenderloin and crab in tarragon butter, and other well-done "new American" entrees. Appetizers include chilled smoked salmon, crab au gratin, cheese puffs with tomato and basil coulis, and homemade champagne scallop soup. A small cafe on the ground floor offers soups, sandwiches and other light bites. Work up an appetite at the Central Market and come on over. *Moderate. Lunch Mon–Sat 11am–2:30pm; dinner Sun–Mon 5pm–9pm, Tue–Sat 5pm–10pm; Sunday brunch 11am–2pm. Bar and wine list. Reservations recommended. All major credit cards.*

Monk's Tunic

18 West Orange Street, Lancaster, PA 17603. Tel: 717-399-9121.

Poetry is scribbled on the windows and art adorns the brick walls of this hip downtown cafe. There's a busy schedule of live performances, including folk, jazz and rock, as well as discussion groups and poetry readings. Muffins, salads and other light bites are good for a midday or late-night nosh. *Budget. Tue–Thu 11am–3pm and 5pm–11pm; Fri–Sat 11am–3pm and 5pm–1am. Hours vary; call for exact schedule. No credit cards.*

Old Greenfield Inn

595 Greenfield Road, Lancaster, PA 17601. Tel: 717-393-0668.

Incurable romantics should ask for a table in the cozy wine cellar, on the second-floor balcony or near the stone hearth at this renovated 18th-century farmhouse with contemporary touches like pastel linens, fica trees and airy cathedral ceilings. The menu focuses on an assortment of American and Continental dishes, including rack of lamb dijonaise, Cajun beef and shrimp, filet mignon, and soft-shell crab. Desserts like pecan pie, citrus cheesecake and sundaes with homemade ice cream are worth waiting for. Dining on a pretty brick patio is available in warm weather. *Moderate. Lunch Tue–Sat 11am–2pm; dinner Mon–Sat 5pm–10pm; breakfast Sat–Sun 8am–11am; Sun brunch 11am–2pm. Bar and wine list. Reservations recommended. All major credit cards.*

Portofino

254 East Frederick Street, Lancaster, PA. Tel: 717-394-1635.

Creative Italian cuisine is the specialty at this contemporary

Lancaster skyline from the Lord's House of Prayer.

neighborhood eatery on the east side of town. Well-prepared entrees like smoked salmon and trout tortellini, seafood gnocchi, and veal Madagascar with shiitake mushrooms, sun-dried tomatoes and brandy demiglaze are served by snappily dressed waiters at sleek, black, lamp-lit tables. Classic dishes like veal Parmigiana and gnocchi Bolognese are quite good, too. Thrifty diners can take advantage of numerous weeknight specials and half-portions of pasta. *Moderate. Lunch Daily 11am–5pm; dinner 5pm–10pm. Bar and wine list. Reservations recommended. AE, Dis, MC, V.*

★ Pressroom
26–28 West King Street, Lancaster, PA 17603. Tel: 717-399-5400.

Owned by the same folks who run Lancaster's daily newspapers, the Pressroom is a classy, congenial bar and restaurant and a popular hangout for journalists. The historic Steinman Hardware Building, with its brick walls, high ceilings and etched glass, creates an airy warehouse-like atmosphere for a variety of satisfying dishes. Dinner entrees include hearty dishes like filet mignon, lump crab cakes, and shrimp and garlic sausage over basil fettuccine. Overstuffed sandwiches have comic-page names like "Dagwood" and "Andy Capp." Inventive pasta combinations, deep-dish pizzas and "frizzled" onion rings are favorites for lunch or light dinner. Outdoor dining is available in lovely Steinman Park in warm weather. *Moderate. Lunch Tue–Sat 11:30am–3:30pm; dinner Tue–Thu 4:45pm–9:30pm, Fri–Sat*

5pm–10:30pm. Bar and wine list. Reservations recommended. All major credit cards.

Quips Pub
457 New Holland Avenue, Lancaster, PA 17602. Tel: 717-397-3903.

Quips offers the style and taste of merry old England in a congenial pub setting. English favorites like meat pies, fish and chips, and "bangers and mash" are the staples here. You'll also find burgers, sarni, salads, and a selection of more ambitious fare like seafood with linguine in saffron butter broth, stew en croute (scallops and lobster with sherry bisque in a puff pastry crust), and salmon with a creamy cognac and raspberry sauce. If a postprandial game of darts is your cup of tea, then by all means indulge. Afterwards, you can quench your thirst with one of the many draught lagers, stouts or ales. *Moderate. Dinner Mon–Sat 5pm–10pm (bar 4pm–2am). Reservations recommended. All major credit cards.*

Sanford's
37 East Orange Street, Lancaster, PA 17603. Tel: 717-290-1833.

Kitsch is king at Sanford's. Visitors are greeted by a large Jolly Green Giant. There are board games under glass-top tables. Shelves are crammed with the sort of ceramic figurines that your grandma used to collect. And condiments hang in baskets over each table. Amid the clutter, you'll find a variety of good Cajun and Southern favorites – blackened chicken salad, jambalaya, red and white chili, po'boys and meat loaf – as well as a few local specialties like chicken and waffles, and oyster pie. There are plenty of appetizers and salads, and a wide selection of tequila and beer at the bar. *Moderate. Lunch Mon–Fri 11:30am–2pm; dinner Sun–Thu 5pm–midnight, Fri–Sat 5pm–2am. Bar. Reservations recommended. Dis, MC, V.*

Stockyard Inn
1147 Lititz Pike (Route 501), Lancaster, PA 17601.
Tel: 717-394-7975.

There's nothing "nouvelle" about this popular steakhouse, set next to the Union Stockyards in a rambling old farmhouse once owned by President James Buchanan. There are no fancy sauces or fussy preparations, just thick slabs of prime rib, sirloin and filet mignon as well as lamb chops, broiled lobster, salmon and a few other hearty selections. A good choice for the meat-and-potatoes crowd. *Moderate–expensive. Mon 4pm–9pm, Tue–Thu 11:30am–9pm, Fri 11:30am–9:30pm, Sat 4pm–9:30pm. Bar and wine list. Reservations recommended. AE, MC, V.*

Strawberry Hill
128 West Strawberry Street, Lancaster, PA. Tel: 717-299-9910.

The wine cellar is packed with more than a thousand selections at this fine downtown restaurant, winner of the Wine Spectator Award of Excellence. The menu is designed to accent the wines with well-prepared but fairly straightforward dishes like filet mignon, chicken confit, salmon Gran Marnier and a variety of pasta. A lighter bistro menu is also available. After dinner, you can try one of 40 single malt

scotches or 30 cognacs, or light up a premium cigar. Exposed brick walls, old barn siding and a crackling fire give the place a historic feeling. Diners can tap their toes to live jazz on Sunday evening. *Moderate–expensive. Daily 5pm–2am. Bar and extensive wine list. Reservations preferred. All major credit cards.*

Taj Mahal
2080 Bennett Avenue, Lancaster, PA 17603. Tel: 717-295-1434.

This is a pleasant place to sample well-prepared Indian specialties. Greenhorns can start with a combination of appetizers – pakora (chicken and vegetable fritters), samosa (vegetable turnovers) and seekh kabab (grilled lamb and herbs) – then move on to a fairly mild dish like chicken tandoori, which is marinated in yogurt and spices and baked in a clay oven. More adventurous diners can try vindaloo, a spicy curry with lamb or chicken; reshmi kabab, ground lamb and spices finished in a tandoor oven; shahi paneer, chunks of homemade cheese sauteed in ginger, garlic, cashews, raisins and a creamy tomato sauce; and a variety of vegetarian dishes. *Moderate. Lunch buffet Mon–Sat 11:30am–2:30pm; dinner Sun–Thu 5pm–10pm, Fri–Sat 5pm–10:30pm; Sunday brunch noon–3pm. Wine list. Reservations recommended. All major credit cards.*

Tony Wang's
2217 Lincoln Highway East (Route 30), Lancaster, PA 17602. Tel: 717-399-1915.

Voted "best Chinese restaurant" several years in a row by *Lancaster County Magazine,* this unassuming little place serves all the usual dishes at an unusual level of quality. Customers are served at about 20 linen-clad tables and can watch the chefs work behind a plate-glass window while they wait for their meals. Located across from the Tanger Outlet Center, it makes a filling and inexpensive stop after a long afternoon of shopping. *Budget–moderate. Lunch Mon–Thu 11:30am–10pm, Fri– Sat 11:30am–11pm, Sun noon– 10pm (last seating is 45 minutes before closing).* BYOB. *Reservations accepted. AE, MC, V.*

Wish You Were Here

108 West Orange Street, Lancaster, PA 17603. Tel: 717-299-5157.

Tucked away in an old row house, this bistro/luncheonette has a comfortable, quirky style. The food is simple, satisfying and well-prepared. Sandwiches are offered on ten kinds of bread. Salads are fresh, desserts sinful. There's a real soda fountain, too. Be sure to ask about the soups of the day. They may be as familiar as tomato basil or as exotic as African peanut with chicken and ginger or Indian lentil with beef. Customers have a choice of three settings: a nostalgic, no-frills luncheonette; a casual downstairs dining room; and a splashy, postmodern room with exposed plumbing and paint-splattered chairs. Outdoor seating is available in warm weather. *Budget–moderate. Wed–Sun 8am–2pm. Reservations recommended. MC, V.*

What to Do

ATTRACTIONS

Central Market

Penn Square, Lancaster, PA 17603. Tel: 717-291-4723.

A market has been held at this spot since the 1730s. The present building was erected in 1889 and is now listed on the National Register of Historic Places. More than 80 stands sell Lancaster produce, meats, cheeses, baked goods, sweets, crafts and more. Don't leave town without stopping by. *Tue and Fri 6am–4:30pm, Sat 6am–2pm.*

Demuth House and Gardens

120 East King Street, Lancaster, PA 17602. Tel: 717-299-9940.

The home and studio of artist Charles Demuth, with a garden and gallery of his work. *Tue–Sat 10am–4pm, Sun 1pm–4pm. Donation suggested.*

Hands-On House Children's Museum

2380 Kissel Hill Road, Lancaster, PA 17601. Tel: 717-569-5437.

The eight interactive exhibits at this museum are designed to stimulate the imagination of young children and adults. A great rainy day activity. *Tue–Thu 11am–4pm, Fri 11am– 8pm, Sat 10am–5pm, Sun noon– 5pm. $4 adults and children.*

Heritage Center Museum of Lancaster County

King and Queen Streets, Lancaster, PA 17603. Tel: 717-299-6440.

A fine collection of Lancaster County art from the 18th and 19th century, including quilts, iron work, fraktur, furniture, wood carving and other folk art. The museum is in the handsome Old City Hall and adjoining Masonic Lodge. *May–Dec. Tue–Sat 10am–5pm. Free admission.*

Historic Lancaster Walking Tour

Information Center, Southern Market House, 100 South Queen Street, Lancaster, PA 17603. Tel: 717-392-1776.

An informative 90-minute tour of downtown Lancaster's historic district. A pamphlet for self-guided tours is also available. *Apr–Oct Mon–Sat 10am and 1:30pm, Sun 1:30pm, or by reservation. $5 adults, $3 seniors, $1 children.*

Lancaster Museum of Art

135 North Lime Street, Lancaster, PA 17602. Tel: 717-394-3497.

The museum has recently acquired exhibit space in a handsome old 19th-century mansion and will be showing a variety of work from traveling shows and the permanent collection. *Mon–Sat 10am–4pm, Sun noon–4pm. Donation suggested.*

Lancaster Newspaper Newseum

28 South Queen Street, Lancaster, PA 17603. Tel: 717-291-8600.

Viewed from the sidewalk, the exhibit traces the history of the press over the centuries.

Landis Valley Museum

2451 Kissel Hill Road, Lancaster, PA 17601. Tel: 717-569-0401.

History comes to life at this collection of historic buildings and tools, depicting the life of rural Pennsylvania Germans in the 18th and 19th century. Inquire about the schedule of craft demonstrations and other special events, including a wonderful harvest festival and Christmas celebration. *Tue–Sat 9am–5pm, Sun noon–5pm. $5 adults, $3 children (age 6–12).*

North Museum of Natural History and Science

Franklin and Marshall College, Lancaster, PA 17604. Tel: 717-291-3941.

Exhibits cover everything from Egyptian and American Indian artifacts to regional plants, animals and geology. Planetarium shows are offered on weekends. *Tue–Sat 9am–5pm, Sun 1:30pm–5pm. Planetarium $2.*

Rock Ford Plantation and Kauffman Museum

Lancaster County Central Park, 881 Rockford Road, Lancaster, PA 17608-0264. Tel: 717-392-7223.

A Georgian mansion built about 1794 by Edward Hand, Washington's adjutant general, and now fully restored in period style. The Kauffman Museum features a collection of 18th- and early-19th-century decorative arts in a reconstructed barn on the property. *Apr–Oct Tue–Fri 10am–4pm, Sun noon–4pm (last tour at 3pm). $4.50 adults, $3.50 seniors, $2.50 children (age 6–12).*

Pennsylvania Dutch fraktur exhibited at the Heritage Center Museum.

Rothman Gallery

Franklin and Marshall College,
Steinman College Center,
700 College Avenue, Lancaster, PA
17603. Tel: 717-291-3911.

The exhibits are drawn from the college's permanent collection and are divided into three segments: American decorative arts, Pennsylvania folk art from the mid-19th century, and a collection of fine art, including many contemporary pieces. *Tue–Fri 11:30am–4:30pm, Sat–Sun 12:30pm–4:30pm.*

Wheatland

1120 Marietta Avenue (Route 23),
Lancaster, PA 17603.
Tel: 717-392-8721.

Costumed guides show visitors around the Federal mansion of President James Buchanan, built in 1828 and furnished with many original possessions. *Apr–Nov 10am–4pm; candlelight tours are offered in early December $5.50 adults, $4.50 seniors, $3.50 students (age 12–18), $1.75 children (age 6–11).*

ARTS & ENTERTAINMENT

Dutch Apple Dinner Theatre

510 Centerville Road, Lancaster,
PA 17601-1306. Tel: 717-898-1900.

Broadway favorites like *South Pacific, The Unsinkable Molly Brown* and *Cabaret* are accompanied by a full dinner buffet. *Tue–Sun. $26.50–$33.*

Fulton Opera House

12 North Prince Street, Lancaster,
PA 17603. Tel: 717-397-7425.

Built in 1852, this beautiful Victorian theater presents a variety of cultural events, including performances by the Lancaster Symphony Orchestra, Lancaster Opera Company, Pennsylvania Academy of Music, and the Actors' Company of Pennsylvania, including a series of Broadway hits like *Annie, Pippin* and *Fiddler on the Roof* as well as original productions and children's shows. Inquire about dining and theater packages. *Call for schedule and ticket prices.*

NIGHTLIFE

Blue Star
602 West King Street, Lancaster, PA 17603. Tel: 717-397-9592.

A bar and nightclub with a busy schedule of live rock, funk, blues and dance music. *Mon 4pm–2am, Tue–Sat noon–2am.*

Chameleon Club
223 North Water Street, Lancaster, PA 17603. Tel: 717-393-7133.

Joan Osborne, Jimmy Cliff, Buckwheat Zydeco and Branford Marsalis are just a few of the big acts that have appeared at this large nightclub in the last few years, not to mention dozens of local bands, many of them rising stars. *Inquire about hours and ticket prices.*

The Village
205 North Christian Street, Lancaster, PA 17603. Tel: 717-397-5000.

A dark and beery nightclub with disk jockey, dancing and live alternative music. *Inquire about hours and cover charge.*

SHOPPING

Anderson Pretzels
2060 Old Philadelphia Pike (Route 340), Lancaster, PA 17602. Tel: 717-299-1616.

A self-guided tour walks you through this large bakery, which turns out a staggering 50 tons of pretzels every day. Visitors can sample the finished product at the factory store. *Tours Mon–Fri 8:30am–4pm.*

Angry, Young & Poor
140 North Prince Street, Lancaster, PA 17603. Tel: 717-397-6116.

You'll find everything for the headbanger at this funky little shop – chains, leather, military jackets, black lipstick and other punk couture as well as a collection of compact disks and vinyl. It's a good source of information about the local music scene, too. *Mon–Sun 10:30am–7pm.*

Art Glassworks
319 North Queen Street, Lancaster, PA 17603. Tel: 717-394-4133.

A collection of art glass, including stained-glass panels, jewelry, vessels, sculpture and paperweights. *Mon–Tue 10am–6pm, Wed 10am–9pm, Thu–Fri 10am–6pm, Sat 10am–5pm.*

Book Bin Bookstore
14 West Orange Street, Lancaster, PA 17603. Tel: 717-392-6434.

A large collection of used and out-of-print books in a tidy, well-organized shop. *Mon–Tue and Thu–Fri 10am–6pm, Wed 10am–9pm, Sat 10am–5pm, Sun noon–5pm.*

Book Haven
146 North Prince Street, Lancaster, PA 17603. Tel: 717-393-0920.

More than 100,000 used and rare books, including a solid collection of local history and German-American titles. *Mon–Tue and Thu–Fri 10am–5pm, Wed 10am–9pm, Sat 10am–4pm.*

Borders Book Shop
940 Plaza Boulevard, Lancaster, PA 17601. Tel: 717-293-8022.

A book and music superstore across from the Park City Mall with more than 100,000 titles, a cafe and a regular schedule of author events, readings and performances. *Mon–Sat 9am–11pm, Sun 9am–9pm.*

Central Market Art Company
15 West King Street, Lancaster, PA 17603. Tel: 717-392-4466.

A small gallery featuring the work of contemporary Lancaster artists. *Mon–Fri 10am–5pm, Sat 10am–3pm.*

Checkered Past
6 North Prince Street, Lancaster, PA 17603. Tel: 717-299-6220.

A vintage clothing shop with a snazzy collection of retrowear and an assortment of punk jewelry. *Mon–Sat 11am–8pm.*

Chestnut Street Books
11 West Chestnut Street, Lancaster, PA 17603. Tel: 717-393-3773.

A general collection of some 20,000 used and out-of-print books, with an emphasis on history, literature, religion and baseball. *Mon–Tue and Thu–Sat 10am–6pm, Wed 10am–9pm.*

Cross Keys Coffee and Teas
52 North Queen Street, Lancaster, PA 17603. Tel: 717-299-4411.

Stop in for a quick cup of joe or take home a bag of fresh beans and all the accoutrements you'll need to enjoy it, including pots, mugs, espresso machines, cookbooks and more. There's a fine assortment of teas, too. *Mon–Tue and Thu–Fri 7:15am–5:30pm, Wed 7:15am–8pm, Sat 8:30am–5pm.*

Coleman's Ice Cream
2195 Old Philadelphia Pike (Route 340), Lancaster, PA 17602. Tel: 717-394-8815.

A local favorite, Coleman's sells rich homemade ice cream in a variety of flavors, including a few out-of-the-ordinary choices like pink champagne, cranberry and nutmeg. *Summer Mon–Thu 10am–9pm, Fri–Sat 10am–10pm, Sun noon–9pm; winter Mon–Fri 10am–7pm, Sat 10am–8pm.*

Demuth's Tobacco Shop
114 East King Street, Lancaster, PA 17602. Tel: 717-397-6613.

This little shop has been run by the Demuth family (now the Demuth Foundation) since 1770 and retains its old-fashioned charm. Don't miss the collection of antique firemen's helmets displayed around the shop. *Mon–Fri 9am–5pm, Sat 9am–3pm.*

Here To Timbuktu
46 North Prince Street, Lancaster, PA 17603. Tel: 717-293-8595.

An eclectic and arty collection of books, cards, stationery, clothing, jewelry, toys and more. A good spot for fun, one-of-a-kind gifts. *Mon–Tue and Thu–Fri 10am–6pm, Wed 10am–8pm, Sat 9:30am–5pm.*

Lancaster Galleries
34 North Water Street, Lancaster, PA 17603. Tel: 717-397-5552.

A collection of contemporary work, with an emphasis on area artists. *Mon–Fri 9am–6pm, Sat 9am–5pm.*

Miesse Candies
60 North Queen Street, Lancaster, PA 17603. Tel: 717-392-6011.

This shop has been turning out dark chocolate, licorice, caramels, peanut butter meltaways and other fine confections for more than a century. *Mon–Sat 9am–5pm.*

Demuth's Tobacco Shop is said to be the oldest in the country.

Museum Store at the Heritage Center of Lancaster County

5 West King Street, Lancaster, PA 17603. Tel: 717-393-3364.

A fine collection of locally made gifts and crafts as well as books about Pennsylvania Dutch culture and folk art. *Tue–Sat 10am–5pm.*

Park City Shopping Center

Route 30, Lancaster, PA. Tel: 717-299-0010.

A modern shopping mall with five major department stores and more than 170 specialty shops. *Mon–Sat 10am–9:30pm, Sun noon–6pm.*

Provident Bookstore

Lancaster Shopping Center, 1625 Lititz Pike (Route 501), Lancaster, PA 17601. Tel: 717-397-3517.

A chain of large Christian book-shops run by the Mennonite Church; other locations include Ephrata and New Holland. *Mon–Sat 9am–9pm.*

Sawtooth

11 West King Street, Lancaster, PA 17603. Tel: 717-295-3961.

Contemporary quilts, carvings, baskets and other folk art as well as a few antiques. *Mon–Sat 10am–4pm, Sun noon–4pm.*

OUTDOOR RECREATION

Lancaster County Central Park

1050 Rockford Road, Lancaster, PA 17602. Tel: 717-299-8215.

More than 500 acres on the south side of the city, with hiking trails, oak and beech forest, an environmental center, covered bridge, Rock Ford Plantation, gardens, pools, picnic and recreation areas.

Long's Park

1441 Old Harrisburg Pike, Lancaster, PA 17602. Tel: 717-397-8517.

A lake, barnyard zoo, picnic areas and summer concerts

make this a popular spot for whiling away a balmy afternoon.

Overlook Golf Course
2040 Lititz Pike (Route 501), Lancaster, PA 17601.
Tel: 717-569-9551.
A fine 18-hole, par-70 course just north of the city.

SPECIAL EVENTS

June
Corestates International Bicycle Race

Bikers from around the world compete at this thrilling race through the city. Call the Downtown Visitors Center (717-397-3531) for information.

July
Pennsylvania State Craft Show and Sale

A juried show of more than 250 craftsmen and artists at Franklin & Marshall College. Tel: 717-291-3911.

August
LancasterFest

A street fair with food, music and crafts celebrating the area's cultures; call the Downtown Visitors Center (717-397-3531) for information.

September
Long's Park Art and Craft Festival

An open-air event with more than 150 artists, live music and gourmet food. Tel: 717-295-7054.

October
Fall Jazz Festival and Outdoor Art Show

An outdoor celebration at Lancaster Square featuring the area's best artists and perform-ers; call the Downtown Visitors Center (717-397-3531) for information.

Harvest Days

An 18th-century harvest at the Landis Valley Museum (717-569-0401), with demonstrations of traditional crafts and occupations.

December
Victorian Christmas Tour

A candlelight tour of Wheatland (717-392-8721), President James Buchanan's home, decorated in lavish period style.

INFORMATION

Lancaster Farmland Trust
128 East Marion Street, P.O. Box 1562, Lancaster, PA 17608.
Tel: 717-293-0707.
A nonprofit organization dedicated to the preservation and stewardship of Lancaster County farmland.

Pennsylvania Dutch Convention and Visitors Bureau
501 Greenfield Road, Lancaster, PA 17601. Tel: 717-299-8901 or toll-free 800-723-8824.
Mon–Sat 8am–6pm, Sun 8am–5pm.

Southern Market Downtown Visitors Center
100 South Queen Street, Lancaster, PA 17603. Tel: 717-397-3531.
Mon–Fri 8:30am–5pm, Sat 9am–4pm, Sun 10am–3pm.

HIGHLIGHTS

- Strasburg Railroad
- Railroad Museum
- National Toy Train Museum
- Gast Classic Motorcars

Strasburg

Believe it or not, this tidy little town was once known as "Hell's Hole." This was back in the 18th century, when the village of Strasburg was a way station for the brawling teamsters who hauled freight on the Conestoga Road, running from Philadelphia to the western frontier.

The ambience changed considerably in 1790 when the town was bypassed by the Lancaster-to-Philadelphia Turnpike. The place became downright respectable. Local ordinances prohibited fairs within the borough, and if you sold or exhibited merchandise, you could expect to pay a stiff $5 fine. Also taboo was bowling – there was to be none of those "ball and nine-pin alleys" for Strasburgers.

The town was bypassed again in the 1820s, this time by the Philadelphia-to-Columbia Railroad. Local businessmen took the bull by the horns and started their own line. They petitioned the Pennsylvania Legislature for the right to build a spur connecting Strasburg to the railroad. A charter was issued in 1832 for the one-track link known as the Strasburg Railroad. Consisting at first of horse-drawn stock, the line ran smack through the center of town until the advent of steam engines, when the tracks were removed.

Hop aboard the Strasburg Railroad for a scenic nine-mile ride on a vintage steam-powered train.

The railroad was continually plagued by financial troubles, and in 1861 it was sold by the sheriff to a private group. After the financial panic of 1873, the depot and stock were sold at another sheriff's sale for $12,725. Many years later, the railroad was said to be on its "last gasp." But there was still some life left.

Today the **Strasburg Railroad** is one of the town's biggest attractions, hauling thousands of visitors annually on a five-mile, 45-minute round-trip through Amish farmland. Passengers begin their journey at the depot's 1882 Victorian station, where they board turn-of-the-century coaches, including a plush parlor car with first-class stewards and open-air observation cars.

Bypassed by the railroad in the 1820s, Strasburg is now a favorite of train aficionados.

In addition to the Strasburg Railroad, there are three other rail-related attractions and several shops catering to railroad buffs. Across the street, the **Railroad Museum of Pennsylvania** houses one of the country's largest collections of locomotives and passenger coaches, from 19th-century steam engines to modern streamliners. Visitors can enter the cab of a steam locomotive and get to see what the state room of a private car looks like. The nearby **Choo Choo Barn** has a 1,700-square-foot model of Pennsylvania Dutch Country with working trains. And the **National Toy Train**

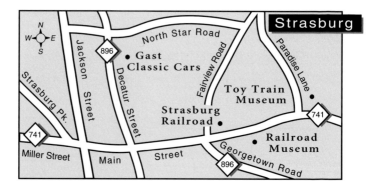

Museum, about a mile away on Paradise Lane, features hundreds of antique and contemporary model locomotives and has five huge layouts operated by push button.

Strasburg is also well-known for its many historic buildings. On a single block of Main Street, for example, you'll find several log cabins built in the mid-1700s, an 18th-century tavern (101 East Main Street) where horsemen could ride through the front door right up to the bar, a handsome Georgian church (St. Michael's Lutheran, 44 East Main Street) with a Revolution-

era cemetery, and a Victorian bank (2 East Main Street) built with Italianate flourishes about 1870. There are dozens of other noteworthy structures. The Strasburg Heritage Society provides information on a self-guided walking tour.

You'll also find several attractions just outside of town on Route 896, including **Gast Classic Motorcars**, with more than 50 antique, classic and high-performance autos; **Sight & Sound Entertainment Centre**, showcasing Christian dramas on a wrap-around stage; **Living Waters Theatre**, billed as a "special effects" theater with laser technology and a live cast; and the **Amish Village**, featuring a guided tour of an Old Order Amish farmhouse. For more information, stop at the visitor center at the Historic Strasburg Inn, about a half-mile north of town on Route 896.

Where to Stay

Historic Strasburg Inn

Route 896, Strasburg, PA 17579.
Tel: 717-687-7691 or toll-free
800-872-0201. Fax: 717-687-7691.

Not historic per se but a faithful recreation of an 18th-century property that once stood in the village of Strasburg, the inn offers lodging and dining on a 58-acre property surrounded by scenic farmland. The inn itself has 101 rooms ranging in size and style from standard hotel accommodations with two double beds and a large deluxe room with a king bed to a bridal suite with an ornate four-poster canopy bed, giant Jacuzzi and fireplace. A free buffet breakfast is offered at the Washington House restaurant, designed in classic Georgian style with stolid brick walls and a cedar shingle roof. The adjoining By George Tavern serves casual fare and a wide selection of English ales. Special events at the inn include an annual hot-air balloon festival, a summer craft fair and exhibitions of antique currency and classic cars. Outdoor concerts are occasionally held on the grounds, and hot-air balloon and carriage rides can be arranged daily. *Rates: $89–$219 double occupancy; three-night minimum preferred on holidays. Free accommodations for children 12 years and younger; dogs permitted. Amenities: 101 rooms with private bath, air conditioning, telephones and cable television; some suites with Jacuzzi and fireplace. Outdoor pool and Jacuzzi, two ponds, garden, patio, fitness room, arcade, badminton, volleyball, basketball; massage by appointment; restaurant, tavern, gift shop; banquet and conference facilities for up to 500 people; parking. All major credit cards.*

Neffdale Farm

610 Strasburg Road (Route 741),
Paradise, PA 17562.
Tel: 717-687-7837.

Staying at Neffdale Farm is a little like visiting your grandmother's house in the country. Acres of cornfields and pasture surround the two modest houses, one of which is next to a barn filled with dairy cows waiting to be milked each morning. The six rooms (three in each house) are simply but comfortably furnished. Don't expect frills and ruffles or fancy antiques. Breakfast isn't provided either. But then, you pay less than half of what most bed-and-breakfasts are asking. Guests are welcome to help feed the calves, sweep the barn and do other chores. But don't expect to milk the cows; it's all done by machine. This is clearly not the place for a romantic getaway, but it's a good option if you're traveling on a budget and want to get a closeup look at farm life, and kids may get a kick out of it. *Rates: $34–$42 double occupancy; two- or three-night minimum on holidays, two-night minimum on October weekends. Children are welcome; no pets. Amenities: six rooms with air conditioning; three rooms with private bath; three rooms with television. Parking. No credit cards.*

Rayba Acres
183 Black Horse Road, Paradise,
PA 17562. Tel: 717-687-6729.
Fax: 717-687-8386

City slickers can get a taste of
farm life at this 100-acre dairy
and poultry operation outside
Strasburg. Guests stay at two
houses. The first is a plush, new
contemporary home with four
large bedrooms simply but
comfortably furnished with
queen- or king-sized beds,
pullout sofas, television,
carpeting and colonial
reproductions.

An additional six bedrooms
(four with shared bathroom) are
in a modest 1863 farmhouse at
the end of a long driveway near
the barn. Guests are welcome
to lounge in two gazebos, tour
the property, even try their hand
at milking a cow. The farm has
been in the same family for six
generations and the staff is happy

to answer questions or take a few minutes to show guests around. Breakfast is not included, but Strasburg restaurants are only minutes away. Tables, a refrigerator and microwave are available in the guest lounge for those staying at the new house. *Rates: $37–$58 double occupancy; two-night minimum on weekends, three-night minimum on holidays. Children are welcome; no pets. Amenities: 10 rooms with air conditioning, telephone and television; six rooms with private bath. Garden, patio, playground equipment, parking. MC, V.*

Red Caboose Motel

P.O. Box 303, Route 741, Strasburg, PA 17579. Tel: 717-687-5000 or toll-free 888-687-5005. Fax: 717-687-5005.

Railroad aficionados will be tickled by this one-of-a-kind motel composed of 39 real cabooses brought here from rail lines as far away as Alaska and the Northern Pacific Railroad. Accommodations are a bit short on luxury, but that's hardly the point. The cabooses offer basic comfort, with various combinations of queen, double, single and bunk beds; some have an extra sitting area. And there's even one – the Honeymoon Suite – with a Jacuzzi. A pretty little farmhouse on the property has been transformed into guest quarters, with three two-room suites cozily furnished in country style. A Victorian dining car operates as the motel restaurant. The lodge also has buggy rides, a gift shop, arcade and a small petting zoo with goats, sheep and miniature ponies. Special packages and events include auctions of railroad memorabilia

and live country music in an old Amish bank barn. *Rates: $35–$99 double occupancy; two-night minimum Jul–Aug. Children are welcome; no pets. Amenities: 42 units with private bath, air conditioning, cable television, microwave and refrigerator, including three farmhouse suites. Restaurant, petting zoo, game room, gift shop, buggy rides, parking. Dis, MC, V.*

Where to Eat

Dining Car at the Strasburg Railroad

Route 741, P.O. Box 96, Strasburg, PA 17579. Tel: 717-687-6486.

The vintage Strasburg Railroad offers a unique experience: lunch or dinner aboard a restored turn-of-the-century dining car. The car is really quite lovely, with its linen-clad tables, mahogany paneling and wood-burning stove. Dinner choices include prime rib, chicken cordon bleu and flounder stuffed with crabmeat. The price covers dinner, entertainment and the train ride. *Expensive. May–Jun and Sep–Oct Sat–Sun, Jul–Aug Wed–Sun; call for boarding times.* BYOB. *Reservations required. AE, Dis, MC, V.*

Isaac's Restaurant and Deli
Route 741, Strasburg, PA 17579.
Tel: 717-687-7699.

This local chain is perfect for a filling, no-fuss meal at a reasonable price. The staples here are soups, salads, pitas and a long list of overstuffed sandwiches named after exotic birds. Favorites include the phoenix – a tower of ham, sliced pineapple and melted provolone – and the yellow-bellied sap sucker – roast beef, melted mozzarella, spinach, tomatoes and Dijon mustard. There are several vegetarian choices, too, including a two-fisted sandwich of green peppers, mushrooms, onions, tomatoes, olives, grilled Swiss cheese and vinaigrette dressing known as the ginko. The dessert menu changes daily and is always worth a try. Other locations include Ephrata, Lancaster and East Petersburg. *Budget–moderate. Mon–Thu 10am–9pm, Fri–Sat 10am–10pm, Sun 11am–9pm. All major credit cards.*

The Washington House at Historic Strasburg Inn
One Historic Drive, Route 896, Strasburg, PA 17579.
Tel: 717-687-9211 or toll-free 800-872-0201.

Although located off busy Route 896, the long, winding drive makes this historic replica seem like a world away. Diners can choose from two settings – the main dining rooms for fine a la carte dining and the By George Pub for sandwiches, salads and light entrees; both are furnished in a pretty early-American style. The dinner menu focuses on such classic French cuisine as steak Diane, salmon en crout, duck l'orange and crab cakes with Dijon cream sauce. The lunch buffet and Friday night seafood and prime rib buffet are great for big appetites. *Expensive. Breakfast daily 7am–10am; lunch daily 11:30am–2pm; dinner 5pm–9:30pm; Sun brunch 11am–3pm. The tavern serves a light menu daily 11am–10pm. Bar and wine list. Jackets suggested. Reservations recommended. All major credit cards.*

What to Do

ATTRACTIONS

Amazing Maize Maze
Cherry-Crest Farm, 150 Cherry Hill Road, Ronks, PA 17572.
Tel: 717-687-6843.

Visitors can spend hours wandering through three enormous labyrinths cut into a growing cornfield. *Jul–Aug Tue–Sat 10am–dusk, Sep–Oct Fri–Sat 10am–dusk; hours may vary; call for exact schedule. $6 adults, $4 children (age 6–11). Inquire about connections with the Strasburg Railroad.*

Ed's Buggy Rides
Route 896, Strasburg, PA 17579.
Tel: 717-687-0360.

A three-mile, 30-minute narrated tour in an Amish buggy. *Daily 9am–5pm, extended hours in summer. $7 adults, $3.50 children (age 10 and under).*

Floating over Amish farmland during the Pennsylvania Dutch Balloon and Craft Festival.

Choo Choo Barn
Route 741 East, Strasburg, PA 17579. Tel: 717-687-7911.

This highly detailed model-railroad display of Lancaster County sprawls across 1,700 square feet and features more than a hundred animated figures and 17 operating model trains. *Apr–Dec daily 10am–4:30pm, extended summer hours. $4 adults, $2 children (age 5–12).*

Gast Classic Motorcars
421 Hartman Bridge Road (Route 896), Strasburg, PA 17579. Tel: 717-687-9500.

Auto enthusiasts will be delighted by this display of more than 50 exotic, antique, classic and high-performance cars. *Daily 9am–5pm. $8 adults, $4 children (age 7–12).*

Living Waters Adventure Theatre
Route 896, Strasburg, PA 17579. Tel: 717-687-7800.

The theater features multimedia productions with Christian themes using live actors, indoor fireworks, fountains, lasers and other special effects. *Call for schedule and ticket prices.*

National Toy Train Museum
300 Paradise Lane, Strasburg, PA 17579. Tel: 717-687-8976.

A world-class collection of toy tin-plate trains spanning more than a century, with five operating layouts, videos and hundreds of displays. *May–Oct daily 10am–5pm, Apr and Nov–mid-Dec Sat–Sun 10am–5pm. $3 adults, $1.50 children (age 5–12).*

Railroad Museum of Pennsylvania
Route 741, Strasburg, PA 17579.
Tel: 717-687-8628.

An outstanding collection of vintage trains and railroad memorabilia tracing the history of the industry from steam power to modern locomotives. *Mon–Sat 9am–5pm, Sun noon–5pm; closed Mon Nov–Apr. $6 adults, $4 children (age 6–12), $5.50 seniors.*

**Sight & Sound
Entertainment Centre**
Route 896, Strasburg, PA 17579.
Tel: 717-687-7800.

Extravagant Christian-based dramas like *Noah* and *The Glory of Spring* are presented at this lavish new 2,000-seat theater, slated to open in fall 1998. *Call for show times and ticket prices.*

Strasburg Railroad
Route 741, Strasburg, PA 17579.
Tel: 717-687-7522.

This vintage steam-powered railroad makes a nine-mile, 45-minute round-trip between Strasburg and Paradise. *Daily Apr–Oct; Sat–Sun and select holidays Nov–Mar; schedule varies; call for exact departure times. $7.75 adults, $4 children (age 3–11).*

S H O P P I N G

Amish Country Crafts
Hartman Bridge Road (Route 896), Strasburg, PA 17579.
Tel: 717-687-9935.

A huge place with a wide variety of locally made crafts, from fine quilts, pottery, furniture and housewares to inexpensive souvenirs. *Mon–Thu 10am–6pm, Fri–Sat 10am–8pm, Sun 10am–5pm; extended summer and holiday hours.*

Eldreth Pottery
246 North Decatur Street
(Route 896), Strasburg, PA 17579.
Tel: 717-687-8445.

David Eldreth and his artists specialize in salt-glazed stoneware and redware pottery designed and manufactured using traditional German techniques developed hundreds of years ago. Handcrafted work includes vases, cups, bowls, decorative items and complete serving and dining sets. *Mon–Sat 9:30am–5pm, Sun noon–5pm; extended summer and holiday hours.*

Moyer's Book Barn
1419 Village Road (Route 741), Strasburg, PA 17579.
Tel: 717-687-7459.

Book-lovers can easily spend an hour or two browsing the collection of old, used and rare books at this roadside bookshop about five minutes from the center of town. *Mon–Fri 10am–5pm, Sat 10am–3pm.*

Old Mill Antiques
215 Georgetown Road, Strasburg, PA 17579. Tel: 717-687-6978.

The three floors of this old brick mill are jammed with a wide range of reasonably priced antiques of various periods, from complete bedroom sets, cedar chests, sofas and wardrobes to toys, wagons and other household items. There's an attached gift shop, too. *Call for hours.*

Strasburg Antique Market
Routes 896 and 741, Strasburg, PA 17579. Tel: 717-687-5624.

This former tobacco warehouse is packed with an assortment of fine antiques, including 19th-century furniture, pottery, toys, dolls, books, glassware, jewelry and other collectibles. *Wed–Mon 10am–5pm.*

Strasburg Country Store and Creamery

Center Square, Strasburg, PA 17579. Tel: 717-687-0766.

An old-fashioned ice-cream parlor and deli with worn wood floors and tables-for-two. There's a full gift shop in the back with jewelry, baskets, candles, toys, books and other country crafts and housewares. *Summer daily 8am–10pm, winter Mon–Sat 8am–5pm, Sun 11am–5pm.*

Strasburg Train Shop

Route 741 East, Strasburg, PA 17579. Tel: 717-687-0464.

Model train hobbyists will find hundreds of items at this large shop at the Choo Choo Barn. *Daily 10am–5pm.*

Thomas' Trackside Station

Route 741 East, Strasburg, PA 17579. Tel: 717-687-7911.

Fans of Thomas the Tank Engine will find hundreds of toys, books, clothes and other items related to the children's television show. *Daily 10am–5pm.*

Zook's Handmade Quilts and Crafts

Route 741 East, Strasburg, PA 17579. Tel: 717-687-0689.

A variety of Lancaster County crafts, with a good selection of oak and pine furniture and handmade quilts. *Mon–Sat 9am–5pm.*

OUTDOOR RECREATION

Fox Chase Golf Club

300 Stevens Road, Stevens, PA 17578. Tel: 717-336-3673.

A fine 18-hole, par-72 course with pro shop and restaurant.

Lancaster Balloons

1085 Manheim Pike (Route 72), Lancaster, PA 17601. Tel: 800-478-4682.

View Amish Country from an altitude of 2,000 feet in a hot-air balloon. Trips depart from the Historic Strasburg Inn and last 30 minutes or an hour; a van follows the balloon and returns passengers to the takeoff area. *Morning and evening flights daily May–Oct. $99 for 30 minutes, $155 for one hour.*

You'll find good deals on handmade quilts in little shops throughout the area.

SPECIAL EVENTS

The **Historic Strasburg Inn** has a variety of seasonal events. For information, call 717-687-7691.

January
Annual Strasburg Stock and Bond Auction and Show

Largest show of its kind in the country, featuring antique stocks and bonds from around the world.

August
Summer Craft Festival

An outdoor fair with more than 150 craftsmen, food and live music.

Annual Pennsylvania Dutch Balloon and Craft Festival

A spirited celebration with more than 20 hot-air balloons, crafts-men, live music, Conestoga wagon rides, petting zoo, air show and more.

October
Dutchland Auto Auction

A three-day sale of more than 500 classic, antique and sports cars.

INFORMATION

Strasburg Information Center
Historic Strasburg Inn,
Route 896, Strasburg, PA 17579.
Tel: 717-687-7922.

HIGHLIGHTS

- Ephrata Cloister
- Artworks at Doneckers
- Green Dragon Farmers' Market
- Antiques Capital USA

Northern Lancaster
Ephrata to Adamstown

*W*hen German-born mystic Georg Conrad Beissel decided to seek God in the wilderness in 1732, he built a cabin on Cocalico Creek in what is now the town of Ephrata. What eventually developed from that act of devotion was a religious community remembered today not only for its austere form of worship but for the art, music and books produced by its members.

Known as **Ephrata Cloister**, the community consisted of three orders: a celibate sisterhood and brotherhood and a married group of householders who lived nearby. The hallmark of the group was solitude and self-discipline. Members spent their days and much of their nights in prayer, work and study, including the writing of poetry and hymns and the making of fraktur. The cloister's press produced a steady output of printed material, too, including *Martyrs' Mirror*, the most widely circulated book in the American colonies.

At its height, Ephrata Cloister had about 300 members. After Beissel's death in 1768, the society began to decline. When the last celibate member died in 1813, the remaining householders

Medieval-style buildings of Ephrata Cloister, founded by Conrad Beissel in 1732. Right, Amos, a 20-foot plaster Amishman, greets customers at Zinn's Diner in Denver.

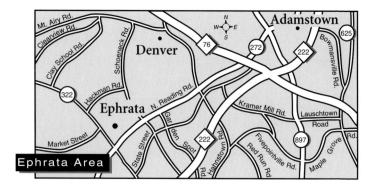

formed the German Seventh-Day Baptist Church, which used the buildings until 1934.

A guide dressed in traditional cloister garb – a white linen robe and sandals – will take you on a tour of the Sisters' House, the Saal or meetinghouse, and a householder's residence, all with steep roofs, dormer windows and wooden chimneys reminiscent of 16th-century German architecture. Take note of the low doorways, designed so that residents had to bow their heads in humility before entering.

Take note of the cloister's low doorways, designed to make residents bow their heads in humility before entering.

Although only three buildings are on the guided tour, many others are open for self-guided browsing. You can also walk among the graves in God's Acre Cemetery, where many members, including Beissel, are buried. Don't leave without visiting the Solitary House, where you can don your own linen robe and try out the typical sleeping arrangements – a wooden bench 15 inches wide and a "soft" wooden block as a pillow. *Vorspiel*, a musical drama depicting life at the cloister, is performed Saturday night in summer.

When you're done at the cloister, travel east on Main Street to the Victorian Italianate mansion that houses the **Historical**

Society of the Cocalico Valley Museum and Library. Here you'll find a wealth of photographs, furniture and other memorabilia from Ephrata and the surrounding area, from 18th-century tombstones inscribed in German to the World War II medals and documents of Col. George S. Howard, a native of nearby Reamstown and founder of the U.S. Air Force band. Just a few minutes away, in a "sisters' cabin" built by cloister members in 1733, is the **Eicher Indian Museum**, a tiny gem of a place with Indian artifacts from all over the country – Anasazi pottery from Arizona, shell beads from Tennessee, and arrowheads dug up along the Susquehanna River. The museum also sponsors regular lectures and storytelling.

Two other stops to keep in mind: the **Artworks at Doneckers**, a unique gathering of artists and craftsmen who make and sell their work in a four-story shoe factory built in the 1920s, and the **Green Dragon Farmers' Market**, a huge country bazaar with everything from clothing, collectibles and tons of fresh produce to lively auctions of farm animals.

For more deals, head to **Adamstown** about four miles northeast of Ephrata via Route 272. It won't be long before you

realize why this sleepy little town of about 1,100 is known as **Antiques Capital USA**. From commercial antique malls and outdoor markets to quaint homes with handmade signs, you'll find your fill of second-hand stuff and old treasures.

While you're in Adamstown, be sure to visit **Stoudtburg**, the Stoudt family's salute to old Germany. The complex features a microbrewery, restaurant and beer garden that is host to various festivals throughout the year. There's also a 500-dealer antiques mall and a recreated European village where artists, craftsmen and merchants live and sell their wares.

Just across the highway is the **Bollman Hat Company**, maker

of the hats worn in the Indiana Jones and Dick Tracy movies, as well as those worn by members of the U.S. Olympic team.

It doesn't take long to see why Adamstown is known as Antiques Capital USA. Hundreds of dealers descend on the town every weekend.

Where to Stay

★ Boxwood Inn

Diamond Street and Tobacco Road, P.O. Box 203, Akron, PA 17501. Tel: 717-859-3466 or toll-free 800-238-3466. Fax: 717-859-4507.

Named after the gnarled, 180-year-old boxwood that grows near the front porch, this stone and clapboard house was built in stages by a Mennonite family starting in 1768. Perched on a hillside overlooking Amish farmland, the inn is decorated in traditional style with thoughtful contemporary touches. The carriage house is particularly affecting, with cathedral ceilings, rich wood floors, a two-sided fireplace, large skylit bathroom with Jacuzzi, and French doors that open to a small deck. Four bedrooms in the main house are furnished in similar style. The Hunt Room, for example, has a more masculine look, with forest-green and blue wallpaper, a queen-sized pencil post bed covered with an Amish quilt, antique dresser and rocking chair, beige Berber carpet, and a large bath with Jacuzzi. Common areas include a large living room with fireplace and an airy sun room that leads to a flagstone patio with views of the surrounding cropland. A full breakfast featuring hot entrees like crepes Lorraine, French toast or a spicy Southwestern quiche is served at two tables in the dining room or, if you prefer, on the patio. Dinner with an Amish family can be arranged with advance notice. *Rates: $90–$160*

double occupancy; two-night minimum on holidays. Children are welcome; no pets. Amenities: Five rooms with private bath and air conditioning; carriage house has fireplace, cable television, telephone and Jacuzzi. Gift shop, garden, patio, parking. AE, MC, V.

★ Clearview Farm

355 Clearview Road, Ephrata, PA 17522. Tel: 717-733-6333.

An early-19th-century house with two-foot-thick limestone walls, this carefully appointed bed-and-breakfast is surrounded by a manicured yard, pond (complete with a pair of resident swans) and 200 acres of soy and cornfields. Three bedrooms on the second floor are decked out in formal Victorian style with ornately carved beds, rich drapes, patterned wallpaper, medallion chairs and a variety of marble-topped vanities and dressers. Two third-story rooms are a bit snugger and more rustic in atmosphere, with canopy beds, wide-plank floors, exposed stone walls and hand-pegged beams. Bathrooms range from snug to spacious; some have handmade washstands fashioned from antique writing desks. A full breakfast is served in a formal dining room using antique china, crystal, silver and lace tablecloths. The meal may include entrees like eggs over smoked turkey and raspberry crepes, a flaky egg turnover, or Belgian waffles with peaches and ham, in addition to fresh fruit and a variety of muffins or shoo-fly pie. A lovely wicker porch rimmed with shrubs and flowers is perfect for an early cup of tea or late-night brandy. Dinner

★ indicates a personal favorite of the author

with an Amish family can be arranged upon request. *Rates: $95–$135 double occupancy; two-night minimum on weekends and holidays. No pets. Amenities: Five rooms with private bath and air conditioning; television upon request. Garden, porch, pond, parking. Dis, MC, V.*

⭐ Historic Smithton Inn
900 West Main Street, Ephrata, PA 17522. Tel: 717-733-6094.

You won't find another inn quite like this one. Everything is handmade, from the quilt-covered canopy beds and sturdy leather chairs to the door latches which, like many other things here, are inspired by those at nearby Ephrata Cloister. Built in 1763, the old stone inn has eight rooms furnished in an uncluttered rustic style, with fireplaces, wood floors, quilts, fresh flowers and goose down pillows. Bathrooms are spacious, and a few have Jacuzzis. You'll find all sorts of fascinating details: a carved headboard with a cloister-inspired dove motif, a reproduction 1640 Dutch cupboard bed, an 18th-century chevron door, handmade wrought-iron candlesticks, and a style of ornamental stucco known as parging. Accommodations range in size from moderate to a four-room suite with kitchenette, parlor and second-story bedroom. A full country breakfast is served at three fireside tables in the dining room and may include French toast, blueberry waffles, fresh fruit and a variety of baked goods; refreshments are offered in the afternoon. Gardeners will be delighted by the prize-winning dahlias in the yard. *Rates: $75–$170 double occupancy; two-night*

minimum on Saturday and holidays. Children and pets by previous arrangement only. Amenities: eight rooms with private bath, air conditioning and fireplace; three with whirlpool; telephone upon request. Garden, patio, goldfish pond, parking. MC, V.*

The Inns at Doneckers
318–324 North State Street, Ephrata, PA 17522. Tel: 717-738-9502.

There are four inns in the Doneckers community, encompassing more than three dozen rooms. Accommodations vary in size and style, although most have a comfortable country feeling. Many are decorated with the Doneckers family's collection of hooked rugs and colorful hand-painted wardrobes and chests. The 20-room **Guesthouse** is the largest of the four. Rooms range from the Rockford Suite, with stenciled walls, fireplace, two-person Jacuzzi and adjoining library, to the snug but pleasant Traveler's Berth, with a double bed, exposed brick walls and wingback chair. Several blocks away, the historic **1777 House** was once the home and workshop of Jacob Gorgas, a member of Ephrata Cloister and well-known maker of grandfather clocks. The lodgings here include Brother Gideon's Loft, a two-level suite set in the carriage house and decorated in pastel colors, with queen-sized bed, fireplace, Jacuzzi, cable television and mini-refrigerator. The Jacob Gorgas Suite features a two-person Jacuzzi and the original marble fireplace. The **Gerhart House**, with only five rooms, has a more Victorian look than the others. The decor has an old-fashioned feeling – like a visit to grandma's house – with inlaid wood floors, stained glass and sturdy chestnut woodwork. The **Homestead**, former residence of the Doneckers family, is the smallest of the bunch. Melba's Suite is a good choice, with an iron four-poster bed, limestone fireplace, Jacuzzi and bay window sitting area. Christian's Quarters is equally appealing, with Jacuzzi, four-poster king-sized bed, bay window and balcony. Continental breakfast is included. *Rates: $69–$185 double occupancy. Children are welcome with advance notice; no pets. Amenities: 41 rooms with private bath (some in corridor) and air conditioning; some rooms with fireplace and/or Jacuzzi, balcony, cable television, sitting area. Gardens, parking. All major credit cards.*

The Inns of Adamstown

62 West Main Street, Adamstown, PA 19501. Tel: 717-484-0800 or toll-free 800-594-4808. Fax: 717-484-1384.

These two historic houses – the Adamstown Inn and Amethyst Inn – are located on a quiet street a few blocks from Adamstown's "Antique Mile." Both are furnished in high Victorian style, with wood floors, floral wallpaper, rich fabrics and a fine collection of antiques, including several pump organs and a gorgeous grand piano from the mid-1800s. The **Adamstown Inn** features chestnut woodwork and leaded stained glass. The four guest rooms range in size from the spacious Redcay Room – named after former resident Harry Redcay, owner of the Adamstown Hat Company – which has a massive four-poster

queen-sized bed and large bathroom with two-person Jacuzzi, to the snug but cheerful Sun Room, with a bank of windows overlooking Main Street. A couple of blocks away is the purple-and-green **Amethyst Inn**, built in the mid-1800s, with sunny bay windows and wraparound veranda. The decor is similar here, except that all four rooms have a gas fireplace and Jacuzzi. The Cobalt Room is the largest, with an oak mantle, marble-top dresser, sitting room and balcony. A continental-plus breakfast is served at a couple of tables at the Adamstown Inn. *Rates: $70–$135 double occupancy. Children over 12 only; no pets. Amenities: eight rooms with private bath and air conditioning, several with fireplace and Jacuzzi. Television upon request. Gardens, patio, parking. MC, V.*

C A M P I N G

Hickory Run Campground

285 Greenville Road, Denver, PA 17517. Tel: 717-336-5564 or toll-free 800-458-0612.

Tent sites and full hookups with swimming pool, fishing, boating, mini-golf and special events like hayrides, bingo and free movies.

Sun Valley Campground

Maple Grove Road, Bowmansville, PA 17507. Tel: 717-445-6262.

Tent sites, cabins and full hookups, with pool, fishing pond, petting zoo, playground, hayrides, volleyball and other recreational facilities.

Where to Eat

Nav Jiwan International Tea Room
Ten Thousand Villages, 240 North Reading Road (Route 272), Ephrata, PA 17522. Tel: 717-721-8400.

A quiet corner of this large handicraft store is devoted to an informal restaurant, featuring the cuisine of a different country each week. Ask about special events, including ethnic music, dance, festivals, stories and other programs. *Budget–moderate. Mon–Thu and Sat 10am–3pm, Fri 10am–8pm. Reservations recommended. Dis, MC, V.*

⭑ The Restaurant at Doneckers
333 North State Street, Ephrata, PA 17522. Tel: 717-738-9501.

The Doneckers family has transformed a neighborhood grocery store into a warm and inviting restaurant. Dinner guests can choose from two menus, served in a warren of handsome rooms filled with a collection of European art and antiques. For fine dining, there are beautifully presented entrees like chateaubriand, seared swordfish with lobster and crab compote, or veal tenderloin crusted with pine nuts and morels over spinach papardelle. The bistro menu features longtime favorites like wild mushroom soup and a trio of beef, chicken and seafood Wellington. Creative sandwiches abound – turkey, jicama and alfalfa sprouts wrapped in savoy cabbage is a heart-smart choice

– as do intriguing international dishes like salmon filets layered with shrimp and scallop stuffing over lemon dill risotto. Home-baked breads, muffins and desserts are first-rate, and the list of wines and beers – including a variety of microbrews – is extensive. *Moderate–expensive. Lunch Mon–Tue and Thu–Sat 11am–2:30pm; light fare 2:30pm–4pm; dinner Mon–Tue and Thu–Fri 4pm–10pm (fine dining starts at 5:30pm), Sat 5pm–10pm (fine dining starts at 5:30pm). Bar and extensive list of wine and beer. Reservations recommended. All major credit cards.*

Stoudt's Black Angus Restaurant and Brew Pub
Route 272, Adamstown, PA 19501. Tel: 717-484-4385.

Velvet chairs, red linens and pressed-tin ceilings add to the Victorian atmosphere at this restaurant in the Stoudtburg complex. The menu is dominated by thick cuts of beef – filet mignon, prime rib, beef Wellington and the like. There are a variety of seafood and poultry dishes as well as German specialties like Wiener schnitzel and bockwurst rolled in pork loin and served on a bed of spaetzle. The brew pub concentrates on lighter fare – burgers, schnitzel sandwiches, a seafood bar, wurst platters and a few Pennsylvania Dutch specialties. At least nine varieties of beer are brewed in the giant stainless-steel tanks, ranging from a dry Pilsener and amber ale to a dark, full-bodied stout with overtones of chocolate and coffee. Several seasonal brews are available, too. *Moderate–expensive. Restaurant: Mon–Sat 4:30pm–11pm, Sun noon–9pm. Brew pub: Fri–Sat noon–11pm, Sun noon–9pm. Bar and wine list. Reservations recommended at the restaurant; no reservations at the brew pub. AE, DC, MC, V.*

Zinn's Diner
Route 272, Denver, PA 17517. Tel: 717-336-1774.

Both tourists and residents flock to this heavily advertised restaurant, famous for Amos, the giant plaster Amishman that stands out front. The food is substantial and plentiful – pork and sauerkraut, meat loaf, roast turkey, chicken pot pie, Wiener schnitzel and the like. Dessert includes local favorites like tapioca, rice pudding and freshly baked shoofly pie. Restless kids will enjoy a recreational park with mini-golf, batting cages, volleyball and more after they finish their meal. There's a gift shop, too, if you need to pick up a few last-minute souvenirs for the folks back home. A children's menu is available. *Budget–moderate. Daily 6am–11pm. No reservations. All major credit cards.*

What to Do

A T T R A C T I O N S

Eicher Indian Museum
Ephrata Community Park, Cocalico Street, Ephrata, PA 17522. Tel: 717-738-3084.

A collection of Native American crafts and artifacts, including jewelry, baskets and ceremonial objects, displayed in a "sisters' cabin" built by cloister members in the early 18th century. *Daily 11am–4pm.*

Ephrata Cloister
632 West Main Street, Ephrata, PA 17522. Tel: 717-733-6600.

Tours of the restored medieval-style buildings interpret the beliefs and austere lifestyle of this religious community, founded in the early 18th century and known for its original music, fraktur and publishing. *Tue–Sun 9am–5pm; hours may vary; call for exact schedule.*

Ephrata Playhouse in the Park
Oak Street, Ephrata, PA 17522. Tel: 717-733-7966.

The summer season features a wide range of shows, from musicals and comedy to Broadway favorites. *Call for schedule and ticket prices.*

Historical Society of the Cocalico Valley
249 West Main Street, Ephrata, PA 17522. Tel: 717-733-1616.

An interesting collection of artifacts and memorabilia from the Ephrata area housed in a handsome Victorian mansion. *Mon, Wed, Thu 9:30am–6pm, Sat 8:30am–5pm.*

S H O P P I N G

Antiques Showcase at the Blackhorse
2222 North Reading Road (Route 272), Denver, PA 17517. Tel: 717-335-3300.

About 300 dealers exhibit fine antiques and collectibles at this sprawling shop on Adamstown's "Antique Mile." *Mon 9am–5pm, Tue–Thu 10am–5pm, Fri–Sat 9am–6pm.*

Artworks at Doneckers
100 North State Street, Ephrata, PA 17522. Tel: 717-738-9503.

Listed on the National Register of Historic Places, this former shoe factory is now a four-story "imagination factory" with some 30 galleries and studios where artists of various kinds make and sell their work. *Mon–Tue and Thu–Fri 11am–5pm, Sat 10am–5pm, Sun noon–4pm.*

Bollman Hat Company
Route 272, Adamstown, PA 19501. Tel: 717-484-4615.

Looking for a new chapeau? You'll find hundreds of top hats, berets, bowlers, baseball caps, cowboy hats and many others at this no-frills outlet on the "Antique Mile." *Mon–Fri 9am–5pm, Sat 9am–4pm.*

Doll Express
Route 272, Reamstown, PA 17567. Tel: 717-336-2414.

Hundreds of vintage dolls – from $1,000 porcelain antiques to a 1970s Disco Barbie – are displayed in six old railroad cars. *Mon–Tue 10am–5pm, Thu–Sun 10am–5pm.*

The Fashion Store at Doneckers
409 North State Street, Ephrata, PA 17522. Tel: 717-738-9500.

Designer fashions for women, men, children and home, aimed at shoppers with discerning taste. *Mon–Tue and Thu–Fri 11am–9pm, Sat 9am–5pm.*

Green Dragon Farmers' Market
955 North State Street, Ephrata, PA 17522. Tel: 717-738-1117.

A large and lively market with livestock auctions, flea market and some 400 vendors selling fresh produce, meats, sweets, baked goods, flowers, crafts and much more. *Mar–Dec Fri 8:30am–9:30pm.*

Renninger's Antique Market
Route 272, Adamstown, PA 19501. Tel: 717-336-2177.

Old-stuff junkies will have a field day sifting though every category of antique and collectible. The market sprawls across 375 indoor stalls and as many as 400 outside. *Sun 7:30am–5pm.*

Stoudtburg
Route 272, Adamstown, PA 19501. Tel: 717-484-4385.

This huge complex includes the **Black Angus Restaurant** and **Stoudt Brewing Company** (see "Where To Eat"), the 500-dealer **Stoudtburg Antiques Mall** and 100-dealer **Clock Tower Antiques Center**, and a growing complex of European-style shops and homes known as **Stoudtburg Village**. *Stoudtburg Antiques Mall: Sun 7:30am–5pm. Clock Tower Antique Center (717-484-2757): Mon–Fri 10am–5pm, Sat 10am–6pm, Sun 7:30am–5pm. Stoudtburg Village (717-484-4389): Sat–Sun 10am–4pm; call for weekday hours.*

Ten Thousand Villages
240 North Reading Road (Route 272), Ephrata, PA 17522. Tel: 717-738-1101.

Run by the Mennonite Central Committee, this nonprofit shop is part of a network that sells "fairly traded handicrafts from around the world." The work is beautiful and varied, including clothes, rugs, carvings, furniture, ironwork, toys and much more. *Mon–Thu and Sat 9am–5pm, Fri 9am–9pm.*

Ultracar Plaza
22 Denver Road, Denver, PA 17517. Tel: 717-484-0414.

Auto memorabilia of all kinds – toys, license plates, hood ornaments, gas pumps and full-sized cars. *Mon, Thu, Sat 10am–5pm, Sun 9am–5pm.*

Weaver Candy and Cookie Outlet
1925 West Main Street, Ephrata, PA 17522. Tel: 717-738-3337.

You'll find big discounts on all sorts of sweets – chocolate, toffee, hard candy, gummy bears, dried fruits, nuts and other snacks – at this large factory outlet about 10 minutes from downtown Ephrata. *Mon–Fri 8:30am–8:30pm, Sat 8:30am–5pm.*

OUTDOOR RECREATION

Hawk Valley Golf Course
1319 Crestview Drive, Denver, PA 17517. Tel: 717-445-5445.

An 18-hole course with pro shop.

Middle Creek Waterfowl Preserve
Hopeland Road, Kleinfeltersville, PA 17517. Tel: 717-733-1512.

An excellent birding site, with a visitor center, hiking trails, boating and fishing. *Sunrise–sunset.*

SPECIAL EVENTS

April
Annual Antiques Extravaganza

Nearly 5,000 antique dealers from all over the country converge on Adamstown's "Antique Mile" on the last weekend of April, June and September.

Doneckers Gourmet Fest
Artworks at Doneckers, 100 North State Street, Ephrata, PA 17522. Tel: 717-738-9503.

A celebration of fine food with big-name chefs and cookbook authors.

September
Ephrata Fair

A bustling street fair with food, music, crafts and more.
Tel: 717-738-9010.

November
Doneckers Wine and Food Festival
Artworks at Doneckers, 100 North State Street, Ephrata, PA 17522. Tel: 717-738-9503.

A showcase of Pennsylvania's finest wines and foods.

INFORMATION

Ephrata Chamber of Commerce
77 Park Avenue, Ephrata, PA 17522. Tel: 717-738-9010.

HIGHLIGHTS

- Lititz Museum

- Sturgis Pretzel House

- Wilbur Chocolate Company

- Mount Hope Estate and Winery

- Renaissance Faire

Northern Lancaster
Lititz to Mount Joy

*H*istory runs deep in the little town of Lititz. You feel it in the buildings along Main Street, some dating to the mid-18th century, many now listed in the National Register of Historic Places. There's the pristine white house of John William Woerner, community cooper, bleeder and tooth-puller. With the warm glow of candles in the windows, it looks much as it did a couple of centuries ago, save for the addition of dormers on the roof and parking meters on the sidewalk. There's also the 1757 Warden's House, originally built for the mayor. That stone building, the first private home in the community, has been completely restored inside and out.

If you're really into history, head for the Schropp House at 145 Main Street. Built in 1793, it's now the home of the **Lititz Historical Foundation** and the **Lititz Museum**. Here, with an interior clearly updated for its purposes, you'll find an intriguing collection of Lititz artifacts,

including an exquisite 50,000-piece inlaid parquet clock made from 20 different types of wood by Lititz resident Rudolph Carpenter and an amusing collection of 19th-century mousetraps

Lititz was settled by Moravians in the 1750s; the Moravian Church was built in 1787. Above, soft pretzels are a Pennsylvania Dutch specialty.

manufactured by the Animal Trap Company of Lititz. You'll also find what is believed to be the largest collection of hand-held fans in the world, including a mourning fan once used by the widow of Abraham Lincoln.

Most important, however, is a timeline of the town's history, from the first settler, Christian Bomberger, who built a dugout north of town in 1722, to the arrival of the Moravians in 1755 and the borough's incorporation in 1888.

It was the Moravian community that gave Lititz its unique identity. In 1742, Count Nikolaus Von Zinzendorf of Saxony, the leader of the modern Moravian Church, preached at Jacob Huber's tavern a mile north of town. Because of prejudice against the Moravians, Huber's neighbor John George Klein, a Lutheran, refused to attend the meeting. The next day, filled with remorse, Klein traveled to Lancaster to hear Zinzendorf preach and was so moved that he eventually converted.

When Zinzendorf decided to establish a church settlement where Moravians could live and raise their families free of outside influence, Klein offered his entire 491-acre farm for the purpose in 1755. A year later, the town was named Lititz in honor of the Bohemian town where the Moravian denomination was founded in the 15th century.

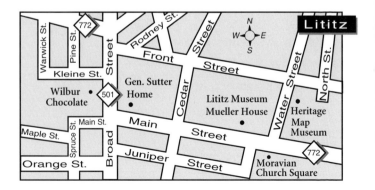

Klein's stone house, built before he sold his farm, became the first in the new town of Lititz. A portion of one of the walls was incorporated later into a three-story brick building next to the Warden's House.

Once the settlement was established, the congregation built a Sisters' House and a Brethren's House to accommodate the unmarried members of both sexes, offer them religious instruction and teach

Zook's Mill Covered Bridge near Lititz.

them trades. Believing strongly that everyone, female as well as male, should read the Bible, the Moravians taught their daughters to read and write.

From the Sisters' House grew Linden Hall, the oldest private girls' boarding school in the United States. The school accepted its first non-Moravian student in 1794 and now boasts a student body from around the world.

For nearly a century, the Moravians maintained strict control of the town, with a body of elders approving the most minute

Moravian elders maintained strict control of Lititz, from the construction of houses to the approval of overnight guests.

details of life, from the thickness of a house's walls to the approval of overnight guests from outside the congregation. That all changed in 1855, when the town was opened to non-Moravians.

Don't miss the historic treasures at the Johannes Mueller House.

Step outside the Lititz Museum and enter the realm of history.
Across the street is the **Lititz Moravian Church**, built in 1787 and
remodeled in 1857. Surrounding it is the beautiful **Linden Hall**
campus, which for a time also served as a junior college.

    Adjacent to the museum is the **Johannes Mueller House**,
home of the town's dyemaker. Visitors are welcome to tour both
floors of the stone house and the attached log section which was
rented out for a time to poor widows. Both have been furnished

after the fashion of the early 1800s. Don't miss the wind-up fly chaser on the kitchen table or the textbooks in the sitting room, hand-copied in painstaking detail by Moravian students right down to the illustrations. You'll also find a wooden sausage maker, an original dye recipe book written by Mueller, and an old mail cart from a time when the house was used as a post office.

With the help of an illustrated pamphlet available at the museum, you can discover some of the other historic buildings on a self-guided walking tour along Lititz's Main Street. Beginning back at the town square, the tour features 17 sites, including the home of **General John Augustus Sutter**. Sutter made his mark not in Lititz but in California. He had gone there from his native Baden to fulfill a dream of establishing an agricultural empire in America. He founded New Helvetia, now Sacramento, in 1840. When gold was discovered there, prospectors overran his settlement and drove him from the land.

Sutter took his family north to a ranch in Marysville, but several years later that, too, was overrun by rustlers and squatters who disputed his titles. Sutter and his wife went to Washington, D.C., in hopes of gaining restitution, but to no avail. The Sutters settled in Lititz around 1871 and he died here nine years later, poverty-stricken and disappointed. The exterior of the Sutter home was restored in 1980, and a hotel named in his honor stands across the street.

According to legend, a hobo gave Julius Sturgis his famous pretzel recipe in return for a meal.

Two blocks from the Sutter home is a can't-miss stop on any tour of Lititz. And with its giant pretzel on the sidewalk, it's virtually impossible to miss. The Peter Kreider House, now known as **The Pretzel House**, is the site where Julius Sturgis established the first pretzel bakery in the New World 1861. As the story goes, a hobo passing through Lititz was looking for a meal when bakery owner Sturgis generously invited him to join the family for dinner. So grateful was the hobo that he gave Sturgis the pretzel recipe.

While you wait for a tour of the house, browse the seven-room antiques and gift shop which, surprisingly, features few pretzel-related items. There are dozens of decorative plates, silver-plated flatware sets, quilts and even a pair of candleholders shaped like boots, much of it displayed in old hutches and on tables in the furnished rooms.

Be sure not to eat all of your admission "ticket" before the tour begins; your guide will need to see at least a crumb as proof of purchase. In the dim light of the bakery, you'll get to stand at a counter, roll your own dough and shape a pretzel. The popular snack, you'll learn, originated in France as a reward for children who said their prayers. In an adjoining room, you'll see the four original brick ovens dating to 1784 and watch as your guide makes soft pretzels. For a small fee, you can take one along on your way out the door.

If you head back toward the square, you can finish your snack just in time to pop into the **House of Unusuals**, where, as the sign says, they sell "antiques and collectibles and nice junque." On either side of the street, you'll find a variety of unique little shops where you can find everything from a corny wooden lawn sign to a Native American headdress.

Venture beyond East Main Street and the historic district for a brief respite at **Lititz Springs Park**, just south of the square on Broad Street (Route 501). Then head next door to satisfy your sweet tooth at the **Wilbur Chocolate Company**. The company's **Candy Americana Museum and Store** features a display of antique candy packaging, tins and advertisements, as well as a video presentation of the candy-making process.

Before you leave Lititz, take a drive over to the corner of North Water and Front streets, just a short distance from the town square. The unassuming red brick warehouse there is home to the **Heritage Map Museum**, a collection of 15th- to 19th-century maps you're not likely to find anywhere else. Even if you're not a fan of history, geography or cosmography, you should appreciate the beauty of these exquisitely detailed pieces of art.

I t's an easy 20-minute drive from Lititz to the **Mount Hope Estate and Winery**, just north of Manheim. The winery is head-quartered in a lavish mansion built in 1800 by Henry Bates Grubb, master of an "iron plantation" established by his father, Peter, in 1784. Visitors are welcome to tour the house and gardens and sample a variety of wines.

The estate is also home to the **Pennsylvania Renaissance Faire**, an interactive medieval fantasy that draws thousands of tourists each year from August through October. Plan to spend a full day at this open-air festival. Highlights include the Queen's court, a human chess

Queen and courtiers at the Pennsylvania Renaissance Faire. Come in costume and get a discount on admission.

Courtesy of Mount Hope Estate and Winery

match and real jousting. There's also a host of showmen like sword swallowers, jugglers, falconers, minstrels and magicians. And don't miss a chance to browse dozens of shops – some under tents, others in quaint Tudor-style buildings – where you can purchase items like pewter goblets, tapestries, Irish saffron shirts and hand-made paper, or watch a glassblower, blacksmith or potter at work.

Continue west to Mount Joy and **Bube's Brewery**, the only intact 19th-century lager brewery still operating in the United States. The complex features three restaurants (including the Catacombs, an atmospheric dining room in the cellar), a biergarten and art gallery. But the highlight is **Cooper's Shed Museum**, housed in the brewery's original barrel-working shop, or cooper-age. The museum features antique cooper tools, some of which are still being used.

Just minutes away, off Route 772 and Musser Road, is **Donegal Mills Plantation**, a once-bustling community founded in the 18th century and now listed in the National Register of Historic Places. A tour of the property includes an original grist-mill and spring house, an authentic German four-square garden, and a grand 19th-century manor that now serves as an inn and museum filled with Pennsylvania German artifacts and Victorian antiques. Don't miss the toy room on the second floor.

Wrap up your tour about six miles away at **Nissley Vineyards** in Bainbridge near the Susquehanna River. Set on 300 acres, the winery encompasses an 18th-century stone mill and sweet stone arch bridge, and more than 50 acres of vineyards. Bring along a picnic and sip a bottle of chilled wine beside a rushing brook or in a sunny meadow. Or visit on a Saturday evening in summer for a romantic concert on the lawn.

Where to Stay

Alden House

62 East Main Street, Lititz, PA 17543. Tel: 717-627-3363 or toll-free 800-584-0753.

Set about a block from the town square, this trim 1850 town house was built in Federal style with a few Victorian touches added some years later. There are five well-kept guest rooms with queen-sized beds, carpeting and heavy wood trim; some have a separate sitting room, fireplace and/or a porch overlooking the small goldfish pond and patio. The largest and most elaborate room is the Rose Garden Suite, which has a columned archway, canopy bed, and a sunny bay window with swags and lace; a bathroom and small dressing area with a daybed are up a narrow flight of stairs, perfect for parents traveling with a child. The Lavender and Lace Suite is also quite lovely, with a four-poster bed, bay window with benches and a small separate living room that opens to a second-story porch. A full breakfast of fresh fruit, baked egg cups, smoked bacon, sweet bread and entrees such as cinnamon pancakes, strawberry French toast topped with pecans, or a choice of eggs is served at a common table in the dining room (couples can request a table for two) or occasionally on the front porch. *Rates: $85–$120 double occupancy; two-night minimum preferred on weekends May–Oct, three-night minimum preferred on holidays. Children over 10 are welcome; no pets. Amenities: five rooms with private bath, air conditioning and cable television; some rooms with porch; one with gas fireplace. Garden, patio, parking. MC, V.*

☆ Cameron Estate Inn

1855 Mansion Lane, Mount Joy, PA 17552. Tel: 717-653-1773 or toll-free 888-722-6376.

Follow a winding driveway shaded by century-old oak, maple and spruce trees for your first view of this splendid brick mansion perched on a hillock above Little Chickies Creek. The oldest part of the house was built about 1805 by a prominent doctor and was later expanded by U.S. Senator Simon Cameron, who served as Secretary of War under Abraham Lincoln. Listed in the National Register of Historic Places, this grand 17-room inn is a symphony of late 19th-century decor, with glossy wood floors, gorgeous wood-work and a tasteful selection of period furnishings that give even the smaller rooms an elegant but dignified ambiance. In the Mary Cameron Room, for example, cheery floral drapes are nicely offset by olive-green woodwork and neutral walls; the room has a king-sized canopy bed, gas fireplace and plenty of space for a sitting area. The midrange Great Room has wood floors, a queen-sized four-poster bed, fireplace and generous bath-room, with lace curtains and Wedgewood blue trim. You'll find smaller and less expensive rooms on the third floor, some under the dormers. Even the staircase and corridors are beautifully finished. On the third-

☆ indicates a personal favorite of the author

floor landing, for example, a large paneled skylight illuminates the striking floral wallpaper in a common sitting area. The dining room and formal library are equally impressive, with just a hint of creosote coming from the old fireplaces. Breakfast is served at small tables on the sun porch overlooking 15 acres of woods and lawn (innkeepers David and Becky Vogt plan to recreate the original 19th-century gardens) and a small stone bridge that arches over the creek. Guests are given a choice of several hot entrees such as eggs Benedict, quiche and omelettes in addition to homemade granola, fresh fruit, baked goods and Belgian waffles. Special events and packages are offered throughout the year, including a seminar for prospective innkeepers and a black-tie New Year's Eve fete with live chamber music, a gourmet dinner and champagne brunch. *Rates: $100–$200 double occupancy; two-night minimum on select weekends and holidays. Children 14 and older are welcome; no pets. Amenities: 17 rooms with private bath, air conditioning and telephone; eight rooms with fireplace. Banquet and conference facility. Garden, patio, parking. All major credit cards.*

Cricket Hollow
240 Evans Road, Lititz, PA 17543.
Tel: 717-626-4083.

Wind past a pond and sheep meadow to this sweet little house with dormer windows, cedar-shingle roof and inviting front porch nestled in a secluded glen by a wooded creek. If you arrive in spring or summer, the first thing you'll notice are the nodding sunflowers, black-eyed Susans, butterfly bush and six-foot Joe Pye weed in a glorious flower garden that wraps around the house to a small lily pond and waterfall. Three spacious guest rooms have a subdued, homey flavor, decorated in shades of pink and violet with king-sized beds, homemade quilts, lace curtains, stenciled walls and other country touches. The largest room is on the first floor and features a Jacuzzi and garden patio where you can be lulled by the trickling of the waterfall and the croaking of a resident frog. Two bedrooms on the second floor have king-sized beds, too; one has an extra single. All three rooms have large modern bathrooms. The family shares its living room with guests. A full breakfast of seasonal fruits, freshly baked muffins, shoofly pie, and hot dishes like sausage casserole and omelettes is served at a common table in the kitchen. *Rates: $75–$85 double occupancy. Children are welcome; no pets. Amenities: three rooms with private bath and air conditioning; one with Jacuzzi and patio; telephone on request. Garden, patio, parking. MC, V.*

General Sutter Inn

14 East Main Street, Lititz, PA 17543. Tel: 717-626-2115. Fax: 717-626-0992.

Built by Moravians in 1764 and known for its "prohibition of dancing, cursing, gossip and bawdy sings," this stately old hostelry in the heart of downtown Lititz is now one of the oldest continuously operated inns in Pennsylvania. Refashioned twice in the 1800s and later renamed in honor of John Augustus Sutter, the ill-fated pioneer who moved to Lititz after his California homestead was overrun by prospectors during the Gold Rush of 1849, the inn has 16 rooms ranging in size from large to moderate, including a couple of two-room suites. You'll find a country Victorian ambiance throughout the property, from the high ceilings, lace curtains and creaky wood corridors lined with Oriental rugs to the ornate headboards and canopy beds, and the antique pump organ and Louis

XIV sofas in the lobby. Breakfast is not included in the room rate, but a coffee shop, restaurant and tavern are open daily. In fine weather, lunch and dinner are served on an expansive, leafy patio overlooking the town square (see "Where To Eat"). *Rates: $75–$105 double occupancy; two-night minimum preferred on select holidays and special events. Children and pets are welcome. Amenities: 16 rooms with private bath, air conditioning, telephone and cable television. Restaurant, coffee shop, tavern; banquet and conference facilities; library. Garden, patio, parking. AE, Dis, MC, V.*

Inn at Mount Hope

2232 East Mount Hope Road, Manheim, PA 17545. Tel: 717-664-4708 or toll-free 800-664-4708. Fax: 717-664-1006.

Built of native sandstone in 1850, this handsome house is set on five acres of woods and lawn on Shearers Creek just minutes from the Pennsylvania Renaissance Faire. Decor throughout the house has a roomy, rustic feel. Simple touches like sheer curtains, hook rugs, cheery floral wallpaper and a few antiques offset the seasoned wood floors, recessed windows, heavy woodwork and other sturdy architectural details. The best rooms in the house are on the second floor. The Parker Suite has a queen canopy bed, plank wood floors, a gas fireplace, and a separate dressing room; an alcove with a small built-in bed is perfect for couples traveling with a young child. Mary's Room is equally charming, with a double bed and old-fashioned clawfoot tub. Three smaller dormer bedrooms are set under low, sloping ceilings on the third floor, with double beds, carpeting and wicker furniture. The rooms may be rented individually with one shared bath or as a single three-room suite. A full buffet breakfast is served in two dining rooms, one with a large wood-burning fireplace. Guests are welcome to lounge on the front porch or in the enclosed second-floor sun room overlooking a massive 300-year-old white oak. A trail leads through the woods to the creek. Discounted tickets for the Pennsylvania Renaissance Faire are available to guests. *Rates: $60–$110 double occupancy. Children are welcome; no pets. Amenities: Five rooms with air conditioning, two with private bath, one with fireplace. Pool, garden, porch, hiking trail, gift shop, parking. MC, V.*

Olde Square Inn
127 East Main Street, Mount Joy, PA 17552. Tel: 717-653-4525 or toll-free 800-742-3533.
Fax: 717-653-0976.

Housed in a stately brick manor with formal neoclassical porticos, this bed-and-breakfast offers five comfortable rooms in the center of town, including a new luxury cottage with huge Jacuzzi and three-sided fireplace. Guest rooms in the main house are of moderate size and are decorated with floral wallpaper, pastel carpets and brass, iron or canopy beds. All rooms have cable television and video; the Garden Room has a Jacuzzi. Common areas include a carpeted living room with contemporary furnishings, a pillared threshold, and an ornate mantle with brilliant white woodwork in the likeness of Ionic columns. A buffet breakfast with fresh fruit, muffins, sweet breads, baked oatmeal, peach cobbler, stuffed French toast, quiche and other goodies is served at tables-for-two in the dining room or, weather permitting, on the back patio. A breakfast basket is brought to the cottage upon request. *Rates: $75–$175 double occupancy. Two-night minimum on select weekends and holidays. Limited availability for children; no pets; the cottage is wheelchair-accessible. Amenities: Five rooms with private bath, air conditioning, cable television and video; Jacuzzi and/or fireplace in some rooms; telephone upon request. Porch, patio, parking. MC, V.*

Rocky Acre Farm
1020 Pinkerton Road, Mount Joy, PA 17552. Tel: 717-653-4449.

Want to give your kids a taste of farm life? You couldn't ask for a better place than this family-style bed-and-breakfast on a working dairy farm in the rolling country north of Lancaster. Guests stay in a weathered stone farmhouse built in several stages starting in 1776 and later used as a link on the Underground Railroad. You'll find a homey, country atmosphere throughout the house – plank floors, quilts, family antiques, hook rugs – with an emphasis on basic comfort rather than fancy decor. Guest rooms, including a full two-story apartment, are outfitted with a combination of kings, queens, singles, daybeds and bunks. One room has a tiny loft with a ladder and space for only one small bed. Common areas include a parlor with a massive stone hearth. A full country breakfast is served

Wheat harvest at an Amish farm.

family-style on pewter plates and bowls at an 18-foot table and may include scrambled eggs and hash browns, waffles, French toast, coffee cake, blueberry pie and tapioca with fresh peaches. But the real fun is outside. Kids are encouraged to bottle-feed calves, feed goats and sheep and play with a dozen or so kittens at the guests' barnyard. They can even try their hand at milking a cow or collecting eggs. There are pony rides, mountain bikes, swings and an elaborate Victorian playhouse. There are special rides on a homemade "train" made of 50-gallon barrels, and there's a rowboat on nearby Little Chickies Creek. *Rates: $79– $150 for families of up to four people. Two-night minimum on weekends; three-night minimum on holidays. Children are welcome; no pets. Amenities: Nine rooms with private bath (one in corridor) and air conditioning; one room* *with fireplace. Petting zoo, playground, game room and other recreational and farm activities. Porch, garden, parking. No credit cards.*

Swiss Woods

500 Blantz Road, Lititz, PA 17543. Tel: 717-627-3358 or toll-free 800-594-8018. Fax: 717-627-3483.

Innkeepers Debbie and Werner Mosimann bring a touch of their Swiss roots to this 30-acre property overlooking Speedwell Forge Lake. The house itself is built in a contemporary style reminiscent of a Swiss chalet. Inside, a variety of European light wood furnishings create an airy, uncluttered ambiance nicely offset by the few traditional reproductions and a collection of antique tools – axes, augers, butter churns, scythes – that are displayed in the guest rooms and common areas. Accommodations are quite spacious, with country French- or Scandinavian-style furniture, including grand four-poster and canopy beds, goose down comforters and duvets, carpeting and modern bathrooms. All rooms have a patio or private balcony with views of the surrounding woods and meadows or, in back, of abundant flower gardens sloping toward the lake. A full breakfast featuring goodies like cinnamon raisin French toast stuffed with wildberry cream cheese, eggs Florentine, finger-link sausages, fruit crumble, muffins, homegrown peaches and homemade jams is served at two large tables near the sandstone fireplace in the combined dining and living rooms, overlooking the garden and lake. Trails are laced through the inn's 20 wooded acres and adjacent state game lands; canoes are kept at the lake. Dinner with an Amish family can be arranged upon request. *Rates: $99–$154 double occupancy; two-night minimum on weekends, three-night minimum on holidays. Limited availability for children; no pets. Amenities: Seven rooms with private bath, air conditioning, telephone and patio or balcony. Garden, patio, hiking trails, parking. AE, Dis, MC, V.*

Where to Eat

1764 Restaurant at the General Sutter Inn
14 East Main Street, Lititz, PA 17543. Tel: 717-626-2115.

New owners have revamped the menu and the well-dressed dining room at this historic hotel on Lititz's town square. Continental cuisine is the bill of fare. Whet your appetite with openers like mussels Provençal or grilled mozzarella, then dig into such classic entrees as veal Madeira, pan-seared salmon, crab cakes, lamb chops and roast duck. Al fresco dining is available in warm weather on a spacious brick patio overlooking the town center. A separate coffee shop serves breakfast and lunch in a more casual setting. *Moderate–expensive. Lunch Mon–Sat 11am–2pm; dinner Mon–Thu 5pm–9pm, Fri–Sat 5pm–9:30pm, Sun noon–8pm. Coffee shop: breakfast Mon–Sat 7am–11am, Sun 7am–1pm; lunch Mon–Fri 11am–3pm. Bar and wine list. Reservations recommended. AE, Dis, MC, V.*

C A M P I N G

Ridge Run Family Campground
867 Schwanger Road, Elizabethtown, PA 17022. Tel: 717-367-3454 or toll-free 800-827-3464.

More than 100 sites for tents and mobile homes (with full hookup) as well as a pool, playground, bath house, arcade, fishing pond and snack bar.

☆ Bube's Brewery
102 North Market Street, Mount Joy, PA. Tel: 717-653-2057.

Three restaurants are housed under one roof at this former 19th-century brewery, now a national historic landmark. The **Bottling Works** is the most casual – a pleasant eatery with stone walls, wooden beams, thousands of empty bottles and an outdoor courtyard. The menu sticks mostly with lighter fare – soups, sandwiches, burgers and the like. About 40 feet underground, the old cellars now serve as the **Catacombs**, an atmospheric, candlelit dining room featuring a variety of well-prepared dishes like veal Dijon, filet mignon, roast duckling and lobster tail served by waiters in medieval costume. A medieval feast is held here most Sundays. **Alois's** is the fanciest of the three. Seven courses of gourmet French cuisine begin with cocktails and appetizers in the Victorian parlor of the Central Hotel (adjacent to the brewery) before moving on to small dining rooms. The menu changes often but may include highlights like veal scallops Provençal, roast duck with red raspberry glaze and Santa Fe chicken. *Bottling Works: Budget– moderate. Lunch Mon–Thu 11am–2pm, Fri–Sat 11am–4pm, Sun noon–4pm. Bar. Reservations are not accepted. Catacombs: Moderate. Dinner Mon–Thu 5:30pm–9pm, Fri–Sun 5pm–10pm. Bar and wine list. Reservations required for medieval feast. Alois's: Expensive. Dinner Tue–Thu 5:30pm–9pm, Fri–Sat 5pm–10pm, Sun 5pm–8pm. Bar and wine list. Reservations strongly recommended. Jackets preferred. All restaurants accept AE, Dis, MC, V.*

Cat's Meow
215 South Charlotte Street, Manheim, PA 17545. Tel: 717-664-3370.

Although the building dates to 1869, the decor revolves around the Roaring Twenties. Period photographs dress up the walls, and mannequins in vintage garb look on from the staircase. Customers can gab over finger foods like charbroiled shrimp, chicken wings, egg rolls and jalapeño poppers in the barroom, or opt for heartier dishes like grilled chicken breast, broiled crab cakes, filet mignon and a variety of sandwiches and burgers. Coffee and ice-cream drinks are a tasty stand-in for dessert. *Moderate. Sun–Tue 11am–midnight, Wed–Sat 11am–2am. Bar. Reservations recommended. AE, Dis, MC, V.*

Glassmyer's
23 North Broad Street, Lititz, PA 17543. Tel: 717-626-2345.

Little has changed at this neighborhood luncheonette over the years. There are spinning stools at the counter, a few patrons reading newspapers, and an old-fashioned soda fountain where waitresses whip up egg cremes, phosphates (flavored soda), malts and ice-cream floats. The food is strictly no-frills – soup, sandwiches, omelettes – but it's a good place for a quick bite, a yummy sundae and a congenial local crowd. *Budget. Mon–Sat 6:30am–2pm. No credit cards.*

★ Groff's Farm
650 Pinkerton Road, Mount Joy, PA 17552. Tel: 717-653-2048.

Groff's takes regional home cooking to new heights. Generous portions of Betty Groff's well-known chicken Stoltzfus (saffron-spiced chicken with cream sauce over pastry), prime rib, seafood and hickory-smoked ham are served a la carte or family-style. Entrees are accompanied by a medley of homey side dishes like mashed potatoes in brown butter, homemade breads and relishes. And here's an interesting twist: treats like chocolate cake and cracker pudding are served at the beginning of the meal while you still have room to enjoy them. The floors of the old 1756 farmhouse creak with age as diners are shown to their tables. A few well-chosen antiques add to the warm and rustic atmosphere. *Moderate. Lunch Mon–Sat 11:30am–1:30pm; dinner Mon–Fri 5pm–7:30pm, seatings at 5pm and 8pm on Sat; Sun brunch 10am–2pm. Bar and wine list. Reservations required for dinner. All major credit cards.*

★ Haydn Zug's
1987 State Street, East Petersburg, PA 17520. Tel: 717-569-5746.

Traditional dining with a touch of elegance is what you'll find at this former general store, built in the mid-1800s and last owned by the eponymous Haydn Zug. The menu focuses on about a

Jousting is one of the highlights of the Renaissance Faire.

dozen meat and fish entrees, which can be combined at your pleasure. A few notable selections include local smoked pork chops with fresh horseradish, veal with roquefort and marsala, charred breast of duckling with Grand Marnier sauce, and steaks that are cut to suit your appetite. To start, try the full-bodied cheddar cheese chowder or grilled portobello mushroom with parmesan crust. Desserts change often, and are always worth a taste, as are the many coffee drinks, liqueurs and vintage ports. *Moderate– expensive. Lunch Tue–Fri 11:30am–2pm; dinner Tue–Sat 5pm–9pm. Bar and wine list. Reservations recommended. All major credit cards.*

Lyndon Diner
665 Lancaster Road (Route 72), Manheim, PA 17545.
Tel: 717-664-4898.

Polished chrome and mirrors add a spiffy contemporary touch, but this is still a good old-fashioned diner. Generous servings of down-home favorites like meat loaf and smoked sausage are complemented by somewhat fancier dishes like broiled crab cakes, Caesar salad and a variety of pasta. An on-site bakery turns out multi-layer cakes, sky-high pies and the sort of tapioca your grandma used to make. Not the place for candlelight and romance, but a refreshing change when you're in the mood for affordable, rib-sticking food surrounded by local folks. A second location, Lyndon's City Line Diner, is now open on Route 72 just outside of Lancaster. *Budget–moderate. Daily 24 hours. Reservations recommended for large groups. MC, V.*

Scooter's Great Events
921 Lititz Pike (Route 501), Lititz, PA 17543. Tel: 717-627-7827.

The menu at this dark and clubby eatery focuses on hearty American fare like Yankee pot roast, barbecue chicken and old-fashioned meat loaf. Other items include personal-sized pizza, six-ounce burgers, generous salads and thick sandwiches. Pasta dishes – including a few unusual dishes like tenderloin tips and linguini with Pilsener beer sauce, and hot penne tossed with romaine lettuce and Caesar dressing – are served in light or large portions. Booth seating is available. *Moderate. Sun–Thur 11am–11pm, Friday and Saturday 11am–midnight. Bar. Reservations recommended. AE, Dis, MC, V.*

Summy House
31 South Main Street, Manheim, PA 17545. Tel: 717-664-3333.

A groove worn into the barroom steps gives you an idea how long this place has been doing business. Built as a hotel in 1876 by local entrepreneur S.G. Summy, the building now serves as a restaurant and microbrewery with a casual, Victorian-style atmosphere. The menu ranges over a fairly predictable selection of light fare – crab cakes, club sandwiches, soups, chicken wings, crawfish – as well as heartier choices like steak Jack Daniels, sauteed pork with onions and Granny Smith apples, prime rib and chicken Alfredo, all served with the signature flowerpot bread. Wash your meal down with one of the beers cooked up by the in-house Prussian Street Brewing Company, specializing in a variety of ales – stout, golden,

raspberry and others – and seasonal brews like pumpkin ale. Brewery tours are given upon request. *Moderate. Mon 4pm–11pm, Tue–Thu 11am–midnight, Fri–Sat 11am–1am. Bar and wine list; microbrewery. Reservations recommended. AE, DC, MC, V.*

What to Do

ATTRACTIONS

1852 Herr Family Homestead
1756 Nissley Road, Landisville, PA 17538. Tel: 717-898-8822.

Guided tours of the historic house and gardens interpret life on a 19th-century farm. *Apr–Oct Sat–Sun 1pm–4pm. $4 adults, $3 seniors and students.*

Donegal Mills Plantation
Trout Run Road, Mount Joy, PA 17552. Tel: 717-653-2168.

An 18th-century mansion and garden listed in the National Register of Historic Places, with an interesting collection of Pennsylvania German artifacts, Victorian antiques and toys. *Call for hours.*

Heritage Map Museum
55 North Water Street, Lititz, PA 17543. Tel: 717-626-5002.

A fascinating collection of antique maps from the 15th to 19th centuries housed in a renovated factory. *Mon–Sat 10am–5pm. $4 adults, $3 children.*

Twist your own pretzels at the oldest pretzel bakery in the country.

Lititz Museum (Lititz Historical Foundation and the Johannes Mueller House)
145 East Main Street, Lititz, PA 17543. Tel: 717-627-4636.

A varied collection of objects and memorabilia tracing the town's development from an 18th-century Moravian settlement to the early 20th century. *Hours vary; call for exact schedule.*

Manheim Country Store Antiques and Museum
60 North Main Street, Manheim, PA 17545. Tel: 717-664-0022.

A complete 19th-century general store fully stocked with original items and preserved as a museum. Antiques are also available for sale. *Tue and Fri 10am–6pm, Wed and Sat 10am–4pm. $3 yearly museum admission.*

Mount Hope Estate and Winery
Route 72, Cornwall, PA 17016. Tel: 717-665-7021.

Built by a wealthy ironmaster in 1800 and later refashioned in grand Victorian style, the mansion is now listed on the National Register of Historic Places and is headquarters of a thriving winery. A tour of the house and splendid gardens includes a formal wine tasting. The estate is the site of the Pennsylvania Renaissance Faire from August to October and is host to a series of interactive theater (see "Special Events"). *Apr–Jun and Sep–Oct Sat–Sun 10am–5pm; Jul–Aug daily 10am–5pm.*

Nissley Vineyards
140 Vintage Drive, Bainbridge, PA 17502. Tel: 717-426-3514.

Tours and tastings are offered at this picturesque 300-acre winery, producing some 24 varieties of wine. Lawn concerts are held June to September. *Mon–Sat 10am–5pm, Sun 1pm–4pm.*

Pennsylvania Renaissance Faire
Mount Hope Estate and Winery,
Route 72, Cornwall, PA 17016.
Tel: 717-665-7021.

An extravagant recreation of
Renaissance times with hundreds
of costumed actors, musicians
and craftsmen as well as special
events like a human chess match
and jousting. Feel free to come
in costume. Great fun for both
kids and adults. *Aug Sat–Mon,
Sep–mid-Oct Sat–Sun
10am–6pm.*

**Sturgis Pretzel
House**
219 East Main
Street, Lititz, PA
17543.
Tel: 717-626-4354.

Listed in the
National Register
of Historic Places
and said to be
the oldest pretzel
bakery in the
country, the
Pretzel House
offers tours of the
factory and a
chance to twist
your own.
*Mon–Sat 9am–
5pm (last tour at
4:30pm).*

*Satisfy your sweet
tooth at the Wilbur
Chocolate Company
in downtown Lititz.*

**Wilbur Chocolate Co. Candy
Americana Museum**
48 North Broad Street, Lititz, PA
17543. Tel: 717-626-1131.

About 120 million pounds of
chocolate and other goodies are
produced at this plant each year.
The museum features antique
candy-making equipment,
chocolate pots, cocoa tins and
a demonstration kitchen where
specialty chocolates are made
by hand. *Mon–Sat 10am–5pm.*

Shoofly pies, whoopie pies and apple dumplings are just a few of the Pennsylvania Dutch treats you'll find at local bakeries.

Winters Heritage House Museum
43 East High Street, Elizabethtown, PA 17022. Tel: 717-367-4672.

These adjacent log buildings interpret the history of the area's Scots-Irish settlers in the 18th and 19th centuries. *Thu noon–5pm, Fri 9am–5pm, Sat 9am–11:30am. Donations accepted.*

SHOPPING

Benner's Pharmacy
40 East Main Street, Lititz, PA 17543. Tel: 717-626-2241.

A real trip down memory lane, this old-time pharmacy has a lunch counter and genuine soda fountain. Where else can you find a 5¢ cup of coffee? *Mon–Fri 7am–8pm, Sat 7am–7pm, Sun 8am–noon.*

Herb Shop
20 East Main Street, Lititz, PA 17543. Tel: 717-626-9206.

An olfactory delight, this little shop is filled to the rafters with herbs, tea, spices, coffee, pasta, sauces, books and more. It's worth stopping for the aroma alone. *Mon–Sat 9am–5pm, Fri to 7pm.*

House of Unusuals
55 East Main Street, Lititz, PA 17543. Tel: 717-626-7474.

A quirky little place with an odd assortment of plates, commemorative platters, mugs, figurines and other "nice junque." *Mon–Sat 10am–4pm.*

Kissel View Farm Bakery
122 West Millport Road, Lititz, PA 17543. Tel: 717-626-4217.

Set on a farm about five minutes from downtown Lititz, this country-style bakery carries pies, breads, ice cream, candy, cookies, jams, herbs and more, many of them made with homegrown ingredients. *Mon–Sat 8am–5pm.*

Roots Country Market
705 Graystone Road, Manheim, PA 17545. Tel: 717-898-7811.

An old-time farmers' market with a bounty of fresh meats, cheeses and produce as well as crafts, household items and farm animals. *Tue 9am–9pm.*

Spill The Beans
43 East Main Street, Lititz, PA 17543. Tel: 717-627-7827.

Hip and homey, this tidy cafe has a plump sofa near the sunny front window and a few little tables for light bites like soups, salads, sandwiches and, of course, a rousing cup of coffee. Ask about Friday night entertainment. *Mon–Fri 6:30am–2pm; 7am–4pm Sat.*

Teddy Bear Emporium
51 North Broad Street, Lititz, PA
17543. Tel: 717-626-8334.

Kids and collectors will love this
little shop, stuffed with about
3,500 teddy bears, including a
variety of fancy collectibles.
Mon–Sat 10am–5pm.

White Horses Antiques Market
973 West Main Street (Route 230),
Mount Joy, PA 17552.
Tel: 717-653-6338.

About 125 dealers display their
wares in a renovated 13,000-
square-foot barn. *Wed–Sun
10am–6pm.*

OUTDOOR RECREATION

Four Seasons Golf Course
949 Church Street, Landisville, PA
17538. Tel: 717-898-0104.

An 18-hole golf course with
driving range and pro shop.

Lititz Springs Park
North Broad Street, Lititz, PA 17543.

A lovely spot in the center of
town with a playground and
shaded picnic tables.

Tree Top Golf Course
1624 Creek Road, Manheim, PA
17545. Tel: 717-665-6262.

An 18-hole, 64-par course with
pro shop, snack bar, night
golfing and regular schedule of
lessons and tournaments.

SPECIAL EVENTS

The Mount Hope Estate and
Winery, home of the Pennsyl-
vania Renaissance Faire, also
presents interactive theater in
the Mount Hope Mansion.
Shows include *The Roaring 20s*
in April and May, *Edgar Allan
Poe Evermore* in October and
*A Charles Dickens Victorian
Christmas* in November and
December.

June
Lititz Crafts-in-the-Park

More than 200 artists and craftsmen show their work at this outdoor fair in Lititz Springs Park,
tel: 717-626-1510.

June–September
Music in the Vineyards
Nissley Vineyards, 140 Vintage
Drive, Bainbridge, PA 17502.
Tel: 717-426-3514.

A series of Saturday-night
concerts on the lawn featuring
big band, jazz and light rock.

July
Fourth of July Celebration
Lititz Springs Park,
Tel: 717-626-7555.

An annual event for more than
180 years, this daylong festival
culminates with a traditional
fireworks display.

August
**Heart of Lancaster Country Arts
and Crafts Show**
Roots Country Market, 705
Graystone Road, Manheim, PA
17545. Tel: 717-898-7811.

HIGHLIGHTS

- Hans Herr House
- Robert Fulton Birthplace
- Wright's Ferry Mansion
- Watch and Clock Museum
- Le Petit Museum of Musical Boxes

Southern Lancaster
& the Susquehanna River

"*N*owhere in this country... does nature comfort us with such assurance of plenty, such rich and tranquil beauty as in those unsung, unpainted hills of Pennsylvania," observed author and Pennsylvania native Rebecca Harding Davis. And nowhere is nature more bountiful than in southern Lancaster County.

In many respects, this is Lancaster as it used to be. Woodlands stretch along the Susquehanna River. Neatly sown fields of corn and tobacco roll into the distance. There are no malls, no traffic, no amusement parks. Just the simple pleasures of land and sky and open road.

Perhaps the best place to start your tour is a few miles south of Lancaster, where Mennonite bishop Hans Herr and other religious refugees became the first Europeans to settle in the wilderness west of Philadelphia. The **Hans Herr House**, built by Herr's son Christian in 1719, is the oldest house in Lancaster County and the oldest Mennonite meetinghouse in the Western Hemisphere. It replaced an earlier log house built in 1711.

Although most of the 18th-century artifacts in the house are not original to

Wildflowers bloom around a country church near Columbia. Right, clock tower at the Watch and Clock Museum in downtown Columbia.

the Herr family, they are based on an inventory of the household taken in 1750 at the time of Christian's death. They include farm implements, a few sparse period furnishings and some clothing.

The Hans Herr House is the oldest house in Lancaster County and the oldest Mennonite meetinghouse in North America.

The most fascinating pieces, however, are the original books found in the room once used for Mennonite services. On a long table sits the care-worn Herr family Bible, a copy of the thick tome *Martyr's Mirror* which documents the persecution of Anabaptists in Europe, and a hymnbook signed and donated by Lancaster County resident Martin Meillin in 1744.

Meillin is famous in his own right as the inventor of the Pennsylvania long rifle, later used by Daniel Boone in Kentucky. His gun shop, possibly the second oldest building in the county, still stands about a mile from the Herr House.

Return to Route 222 and continue south. Although there are plenty of scenic back roads at this end of the county, you can see just as much rolling farmland from this major byway, much of it bordered on either side by lush crops and trim farmhouses as far as the eye can see.

A few miles south of Quarryville, in a peaceful shaded glen at a curve in the road, you'll find the **Robert Fulton Birthplace**. Born here in 1765, the famous inventor and painter is best known for his steamboat, *Clermont,* but he also invented canal machinery and torpedoes. The small fieldstone house is shaded by a majestic sycamore tree thought to be more than 150 years old. To the rear is a neatly fenced 18th-century herb garden. The house and grounds are open on weekends in summer.

Return to Quarryville and head west on Route 372 for a look at the 1,200-acre system of parks and woodlands maintained along the Susquehanna River by local power companies. The routes may be circuitous but are well-marked. A good place to start is **Pinnacle Overlook**, which offers a breathtaking view of the river's Lake Aldred formed by Holtwood Dam. Set at an elevation of more than 700 feet, the site is perfect for picnic lunches, enjoying the beautiful butterfly population, or simply sitting on one of the benches overlooking the river. You can also pick up a brochure here detailing some of the other overlooks, campgrounds and nature trails in the area.

Return to Route 372 and continue east a short distance to **Muddy Run Recreation Park**, which features a 100-acre lake surrounded by 700 acres of woods and rolling fields. Here you can rent a rowboat, a motorboat, even a paddle boat, go fishing or camping, or take a hike and try to spot songbirds, white-tailed deer or bald eagles. Don't miss the visitor center, an educational extravaganza that uses interactive exhibits, videos and demonstrations to explain everything from operating a radiation detector to building

Robert Fulton was raised in a typical stone farmhouse in southern Lancaster County.

a bluebird's nesting box. The center also has a handy, free map for locating other recreation areas and the best fishing spots along the lower Susquehanna.

Continue east on Route 372 to Susquehannock Drive, then follow signs to **Susquehannock State Park**, another fine wooded recreation area with numerous hiking and nature trails, river over-looks, pavilions and playgrounds.

Amish farmers outside of Willow Street transport a load of hay.

To the north, the Susquehanna takes on a different face, that of an industrial giant past its prime. Make your first stop **Columbia**, a 19th-century factory town directly west of Lancaster. Nearly chosen as capital of the United States in 1789, Columbia owed its industrial might to an elaborate canal system that gave river transportation a boost along this stretch of the river.

Columbia's early history is linked to a refined young English woman named Susanna Wright. If you head toward the river at the west end of town, you'll find **Wright's Ferry Mansion**, the beautiful limestone Georgian-style house Wright built in 1738.

Wright's family moved to Pennsylvania from Lancashire, England, in 1714, when she was only 16. The family settled near Philadelphia. As the well-educated Susanna grew older, she developed a friendship with James Logan, secretary to William Penn. Through him, she learned about the commonwealth and its relations with the Indians.

At 29, Susanna became the first European to purchase land along the Susquehanna, where she intended to spread her Quaker beliefs among the Indians. She established a ferry, built roads, planted crops, and operated a gristmill and silk-making shop. She studied astronomy, biology and Indian remedies, and dispensed legal and medical advice to those who settled after her.

A visit to the mansion is fascinating on several levels. For those interested in decorative arts, there's a rare collection of furnishings predating 1755. More impor-

A daring young woman, Susanna Wright was the first European to buy land along the Susquehanna River.

tantly, however, the house shows how this independent woman was able to maintain a refined English life-style in an unforgiving wilderness. From the rare high-post Philadelphia Queen Anne bed to the delicate imported china, it's clear that Wright was hardly roughing it. Although she never married, the mansion remained in her family until 1922. Broken shackles in the attic are one indication that it was also a stop on the Underground Railroad long after her death.

A farm near Millersville; the attraction of southern Lancaster is its rustic beauty.

Just a few minutes away, at Fifth and Poplar streets, is the impressive **Watch and Clock Museum**, which offers a detailed look at the inner workings of timepieces, from the most primitive water and shadow clocks to magnificent wooden cathedral clocks with exquisite perforated carvings. Even if some of the mechanical jargon is over your head, you can still enjoy the sheer artistry of the more than 8,000 items on display here. There's an ornate French clock made of inlaid tulip wood during the reign of Louis XV; an early time clock with a huge cast-iron wheel and pointer that employees swung around before "punching in"; and a sterling-silver and turquoise Tiffany globe clock that actually rotated on an onyx base every 24 hours. Just for fun, you can punch in and out of the museum on a 1913 pendulum-operated time clock.

Drive north of town on Route 441 past two scenic overlooks with spectacular views of the Susquehanna River. Both are part of 420-acre **Chickies Rock County Park**.

A few miles north is **Marietta**, another river town long past its industrial heyday. Dozens of stately Victorian houses were built here in the glory days when the Pennsylvania Railroad fueled the town's economy. Many are so well-preserved that nearly half the town has been declared a National Historic District.

Nearly half of Marietta has been declared a National Historic District.

If time allows, stroll the downtown area for a look at its many antique shops and fine old buildings, including the **Old Town Hall**, which now houses a museum interpreting the town's history. And don't miss **Le Petit Museum of Musical Boxes** (255 W. Market Street), housed in a Federal town house that's been painted a subtle but eye-catching shade of green. Even the sign, featuring a cherubic figure playing the violin, exudes Victorian charm. Among the sweet treasures you'll find here are Swiss cylinder music boxes, a 1910 birdcage music box, musical beer steins, hot plates and chairs, and a magnificent 1896 Regina music box with 27-inch discs. The museum also has a gift shop and gardens.

Where to Stay

The Columbian

360 Chestnut Street, Columbia, PA 17512. Tel: 717-684-5869 or toll-free 800-422-5869.

This handsome Colonial Revival mansion was built in 1897 and is set on a busy street in the heart of Columbia. Five guest rooms are furnished in a casual Victorian or English Country style, all with queen-sized beds, handmade quilts and a few antiques. Some rooms have a canopy bed; three have a gas fireplace. Common areas include a sitting room with wood floors and fireplace, and a grand winding staircase with dramatic stained-glass windows. A full country breakfast featuring pancakes, waffles, egg casserole and other hot entrees is served at a single table by the fireplace in the dining room. *Rates: $70–$95 double occupancy. Two-night minimum on holiday and October weekends. Children are welcome; no pets. Amenities: Five rooms with private bath, air conditioning and cable television, three with gas fireplace. Porch, garden, parking. MC, V.*

☆ Mellinger Manor

1300 Breneman Road, Conestoga, PA 17516. Tel: 717-871-0699.

With its conical turret and wrap-around veranda, this gorgeous Edwardian home looks like a fairy-tale castle surrounded by the graceful rolling farmland of southern Lancaster. Built in 1893 by a local doctor as a wedding present for his son, the house now offers three airy guest rooms decorated with a light period touch. The Turret Room is the largest and most elegant, with a king-sized brass bed, lustrous wood floors, wood Venetian blinds, lace swags and a sunny alcove inside the turret. The Wicker Room is equally lovely. It shares a bath with the smaller and more masculine Civil War Room, which has antique sabers and Civil War uniforms from the collection of innkeeper Bob VanderPlate, an experienced reenactor. Take note of the heavy woodwork, ornamental plaster, etched glass and other architectural details in the foyer and front parlor, which is decorated with a burgundy velvet sofa, oriental rug and year-round Christmas tree. A full breakfast of egg casserole, Belgian waffles or stuffed French toast is served at a large table in the dining room set with crystal and china or, if you want extra privacy, in the more casual breakfast room. Special events are held throughout the year, including a full-fledged Civil War encampment, antique car show, and Victorian weekend with costume ball and no electricity. *Rates: $75 double occupancy. Children are welcome; inquire in advance about pets. Amenities: Three rooms, one with private bath, two with shared bath; Porch, garden, special events, parking. Inquire about credit cards.*

Railroad House

280 West Front Street, Marietta, PA 17547. Tel: 717-426-4141.

The Railroad House was built in 1820 as a hostel and tavern for the lusty men who worked the Susquehanna River and later the Pennsylvania Main Line Canal.

When the railroad came through in the 1850s, the hotel was used temporarily as a train station and was later purchased by Colonel Thomas Scott, president of the Pennsylvania Railroad and Assistant Secretary of War under Abraham Lincoln. Today, the hotel offers 10 guest rooms ranging in size from snug to spacious. Most are decorated in casual Victorian style, some with impressive carved headboards, a few antiques, and balcony. For extra privacy, ask for the summer kitchen, a detached building with plank floors, a queen-sized bed, tiny kitchenette, and small loft with two single beds. A full country breakfast featuring quiche, chocolate chip pancakes, biscuits and gravy, and other entrees is served in the first-floor restaurant (see "Where To Eat"). An a la carte brunch is offered on Sunday. Ask about lodging and dining packages. *Rates: $69–$99 double occupancy. Children are welcome; no pets. Amenities: Ten rooms with air conditioning, eight with private bath, two with shared bath. Gardens, gift shop, conference and banquet facilities, restaurant, tavern, parking. MC, V.*

River Inn

258 West Front Street, Marietta, PA 17547. Tel: 717-426-2290 or toll-free 888-824-6622. Fax: 717-426-2966.

Set in a historic district near the Susquehanna River, this modest clapboard house was built in at least two stages. The oldest part dates to 1790 and was used as a tenant house. A blacksmith shop was added in 1830. Three comfortable bedrooms are decorated with a mix of antiques and fine reproductions, including queen-sized canopy beds, wingback chairs, oriental rugs, wide-plank floors and thick plaster walls. Breakfast features herbs and vegetables from the colonial garden and may include omelettes with hash browns and bacon, French toast and sausage, sauteed apples, sweet bread, fresh fruit and more. Breakfast is served by the fireplace in the dining room or, if weather permits, on a screened-in porch overlooking the garden. Guests are welcome to use two bicycles. Guided river tours and fishing can be arranged with advance notice. *Rates: $60–$80 double occupancy. Children 10 years or older are welcome; no pets. Amenities: Three rooms with private bath and air conditioning, one with fireplace. Porch, garden, bicycles, river tours, parking. DC, Dis, MC, V.*

Where to Eat

★ Accomac Inn

6330 South River Drive, Wrightsville, PA 17368. Tel: 717-252-1521.

Two centuries ago, this handsome stone inn was a way station for travelers crossing the Susquehanna River on Anderson's Ferry. Today, guests arrive by minivan for a taste of fine French and American cuisine – rack of lamb Dijon over rosemary demi-glaze, pepper-crusted tuna with

★ indicates a personal favorite of the author

bourbon-vanilla butter and raspberry barbecue sauce, roast duck with Grand Marnier, and New York sirloin with a Jack Daniels-mustard demiglaze. Health-conscious diners will appreciate the few heart-healthy recipes but may find desserts like baked Alaska, bananas Foster and a wine-poached pear stuffed with ice cream and served in a puddle of chocolate difficult to resist. The ambiance is formal: white tablecloths, pewter settings, antique reproductions, flickering candlelight and a stone fireplace. A screened-in porch has views of the river and is a lovely spot for the popular Sunday champagne brunch. *Expensive. Dinner Mon–Sat 5:30pm–9:30pm, Sun 4pm–8:30pm; Sunday brunch 11am–2:30pm. Bar and wine list. Reservations recommended. AE, MC, V.*

Josephine's

324 West Market Street, Marietta, PA 17547. Tel: 717-426-2003.

Romance is in the air at this fine French restaurant, set in a restored 18th-century log house. A crackling fire, soft French music, rough-hewn beams and candlelit tables create a subdued, intimate atmosphere for such delicately prepared dishes as sauteed chicken breast with tarragon and white wine, thin slices of veal with morels in cream sauce, and duck with pear poached in honey and saffron. Nightly specials take advantage of the freshest seasonal ingredients. Pretty little apple tarts and silky chocolate mousse and creme caramel are even more luscious with a demitasse of strong espresso. *Moderate–expensive. Lunch Tue–Fri 11:30am–2pm; dinner Mon–Sat 5pm–9pm. Bar and wine list. Reservations recommended. AE, MC, V.*

Loreto's Ristorante

173 South Fourth Street, Columbia, PA. Tel: 717-684-4326.

Eleven members of the Loreto family are on staff at this pretty restaurant, including mother Mary, whose homemade sauce recipes have been handed down from generation to generation. The menu features northern Italian fare with a few French dishes like veal Oscar and chicken Leone thrown in. Start with antipasto, escarole wedding soup or steamed mussels, and then dig into an assortment of freshly made pasta, steak, poultry or seafood. Save room for dessert. You're sure to be tempted by the dreamy amaretto cheesecake. Wines include a selection of

Italian, California and Pennsylvania labels, served at linen-clad tables or at the old-fashioned hardwood bar. *Moderate. Lunch Tue–Fri 11am–2pm; dinner Tue–Thu 4pm–9pm, Fri–Sat 4pm–10pm, Sun 4pm–8pm. Bar and wine list. Reservations recommended. All major credit cards.*

Prudhomme's Lost Cajun Kitchen
519 Cherry Street, Columbia, PA 17512. Tel: 717-684-1706.

Jambalaya, etouffe, crawfish, and blackened pork chops are just a few of the Cajun specialties at this renovated 19th-century tavern. Co-owner and chef David Prudhomme shares the family talent for cooking; his uncle is celebrity New Orleans chef Paul Prudhomme. Hurricanes, swamp water and other potent southern favorites are offered at the bar, as are New Orleans brews like Dixie Beer and Blackened Voodoo Lager. Live Cajun, country and folk music several nights a week completes the atmosphere. *Moderate. Lunch Tue–Sat 11am–2:30pm; dinner Mon–Thu 4:30pm–10pm, Fri–Sat 11am–midnight. Bar and wine list. Reservations for parties of five or more. AE, Dis, MC, V.*

Railroad House
West Front and South Perry Streets, Marietta, PA 17547. Tel: 717-426-4141.

This historic inn has undergone quite a few transformations over the years. It was built in 1820 as a hostel for rivermen, and later served as a railroad hotel, gourmet restaurant and psychedelic coffeehouse. Continental cuisine is the bill of fare today – filet mignon, chicken moutarde, broiled lump crab cakes, a variety of pasta and other carefully prepared dishes. Alfresco dining is offered in the rear courtyard during the warmer months. A regular schedule of special events includes cigar dinners, wine tastings, luncheon lectures, oyster roasts, live jazz, cooking classes and more. *Expensive. Lunch Tue–Sat 11am–2pm, Sun 2pm–4pm; Dinner Tue–Thu 5pm–8pm, Fri–Sat 5pm–10pm, Sun 4pm–8pm; Sunday brunch 11am–2pm. Wine list. Reservations recommended. MC, V.*

What to Do

A T T R A C T I O N S

Hans Herr House
1849 Hans Herr Drive, Willow Street, PA 17584. Tel: 717-464-4438.

Built in 1719, this is the oldest structure in Lancaster County and the oldest Mennonite meetinghouse in America. *Apr–Dec Mon–Sat 9am–4pm.*

Le Petit Museum of Musical Boxes
255 West Market Street, Marietta, PA 17547. Tel: 717-426-1154.

A collection of antique music boxes from the 19th century and early 20th century housed in a Federal town house. *Mar–Dec Sat and Mon 10am–4pm, Sun noon–4pm.*

Old Town Hall Museum

22 Waterford Avenue, Marietta, PA 17547. Tel: 717-426-4746.

Built in 1847, Marietta's former Town Hall is now home to a museum that interprets the town's industrial history. *Apr–Dec Sat 10am–3pm, Sun 1pm–4pm. Donations accepted.*

Robert Fulton Birthplace

Route 222, Quarryville, PA 17566

Tour guides interpret the life and work of inventor and artist Robert Fulton at this little stone house about six miles south of Quarryville. *Jun–Aug Sat 11am–4pm, Sun 1pm–5pm.*

Sickman's Mill

671 Sand Hill Road, Pequea, PA 17565. Tel: 717-872-5951.

A historic mill on Pequea Creek built in 1793 and renovated in the mid-19th century. The site also offers hiking, fishing, tubing and camping. *May–Aug daily 10am–5pm.*

Watch and Clock Museum

514 Poplar Street, Columbia, PA 17512. Tel: 717-684-8261.

More than 8,000 clocks, watches and other objects chronicle the history of timekeeping from the 17th century to the present day. *Tue–Sat 9am–4pm, Sun noon–4pm (May–Sep).*

Wright's Ferry Mansion

38 South Second Street, Columbia, PA 17512. Tel: 717-684-4325.

The former house of Susanna Wright, a young English woman who settled in the wilderness here in 1738, now restored and furnished with an excellent collection of 18th-century decorative arts. *May–Oct Tue, Wed, Fri, Sat 10am–3pm.*

SHOPPING

Columbia Farmers' Market

Third and Locust Streets, Columbia, PA 17512. Tel: 717-684-0221.

Fresh produce, meats, cheeses, baked goods and other country items are offered in a 19th-century market house, part of which was used as a jail. *Fri 7am–4pm, Sat 7am–noon.*

John Wright Warehouse

North Front Street, Wrightsville, PA 17368. Tel: 717-252-2519.

An assortment of country wares with an emphasis on cast-iron products – kettles, cookware, toys, lanterns and more – housed in an old brick factory on the Susquehanna River. *Mon–Sat 9am–5pm, Sun noon–5pm.*

Red Barn Market

1402 Georgetown Road (Route 896), Quarryville, PA 17566. Tel: 717-529-6040.

An old-fashioned farm stand with a bounty of seasonal produce. *May–Oct Mon–Sat 8am–6pm.*

Susquehanna Glass Factory Store

Avenue H, Columbia, PA 17512. Tel: 717-684-2155.

Good deals on all kinds of glass and china, from fine crystal lamps and handcut stemware to casual dinner sets. *Mon–Sat 9am–5pm.*

OUTDOOR RECREATION

Chickies Rock County Park
Route 441, Chickies, PA; call
Lancaster County Department
of Parks and Recreation,
717-299-8215.

You'll find great views atop
Chickies Rock, an outcropping
some 200 feet above the
Susquehanna River; the park
sprawls across 420 acres between
Marietta and Columbia.

Muddy Run Recreation Park
Route 372, Holtwood, PA.

This large park on the Muddy
Run Reservoir is a good spot for
hiking, boating, camping and
wildlife watching; stop first at
the visitor center for additional
information.

Susquehannock State Park
1880 Park Drive, Drumore, PA
17518. Tel: 717-548-3361.

More than 200 acres of forest
with gorgeous vistas of the
Susquehanna River as well as hiking and horseback-riding trails.

Tanglewood Manor
653 Scotland Road, Quarryville,
PA 17566. Tel: 717-786-2220.

An 18-hole, par-72 golf course
with driving range, mini-golf,
coffee shop, tournaments and
lessons.

SPECIAL EVENTS

June
**Columbia Craft, Antique and
Art Show**
Locust Street Park, Columbia, PA.
Tel: 717-684-5249.

A juried outdoor show with
dozens of area dealers.

August
**Heritage Days at the
Hans Herr House**
1849 Hans Herr Drive, Willow
Street, PA 17584. Tel: 717-464-4438.

Living-history exhibition with
demonstrations of 18th-century
gardening, blacksmithing, open-
hearth cooking and other
activities.

September
Southern Lancaster County Fair
Legion Park and Fairgrounds,
Quarryville. Tel: 717-786-4884.

A traditional country fair with
livestock competitions, crafts,
food and other down-home
attractions.

October
Bridge Bust
Route 462 Bridge between
Columbia and Wrightsville.
Tel: 717-684-5249.

Food, crafts and live entertainment on a bridge high above the
Susquehanna River.

December
Marietta Candlelight House Tour
Susquehanna Heritage Tourist
and Information Center.
Tel: 717-684-5249.

Civil War reenactment, antique
show, live music and other
events capped off with a candlelight tour of historic houses.

INFORMATION

**Susquehanna Heritage Tourist
and Information Center**
445 Linden Street, Columbia, PA
17512. Tel: 717-684-5249.

CITY OF READING
BERKS
ARTS
COUNCIL
PAGODA
SKYLINE
INC.

HIGHLIGHTS

- Factory Outlets
- Hopewell Furnace
- Kutztown Pennsylvania German Festival
- Hawk Mountain Sanctuary
- Daniel Boone Homestead

Reading &
Berks County

*E*ach year thousands of shoppers answer the call of commerce in Reading, Pennsylvania, the self-proclaimed "outlet capital of the world."

Reading was established in 1748 by William Penn's sons, Thomas and Richard, and later developed into a major manufacturing center. It is now best known for more than 300 outlet stores clustered in various malls and shopping centers throughout the area. The **Reading Station Outlets, VF Factory Outlet, Reading Outlet Center** and **Outlets On Hiesters Lane** are some of the largest and most popular, but there are several others where you'll find discounts on everything from pretzels to pantyhose.

There's more to Reading than big discounts, however. Perched atop Mount Penn on the east side of town, for example, is the **Pagoda**, a seven-story Japanese-style tower built as a resort in 1908 by entrepreneur William Witman. On a clear day, the view from the observation deck is truly spectacular, with the Penns' checkerboard street plan directly below and the Schuylkill Valley sprawling around it.

In the city itself, you'll find an impressive mix of historic structures, from the modest, 19th-century, working-class houses in

The 610-foot Pagoda overlooks Reading from the top of Mount Penn; the structure is listed in the National Register of Historic Places. Above, hex signs adorn barns in rural Berks County.

the Prince District to the imposing Victorian mansions in Centre Park. Here too is the **Historic Society of Berks County**, which features a modest exhibition on local history focusing particularly on the development of industry and the artistic traditions of Pennsylvania Germans.

Just a few miles north, the **Berks County Heritage Center** features the **Gruber Wagon Works**, a late-19th-century wagon factory with displays on the tools and techniques of the trade. Also on the grounds is a short section of the 50-mile **Union Canal** and the nearby **C. Howard Hiester Canal Center**, which chronicles the unique culture of the bargemen and locktenders who made their living on the waterway. Although the canal is empty, visitors are welcome to walk or bike along the four-mile towpath. Just a few steps away is **Wertz's Covered Bridge**, the longest in Pennsylvania, built in 1867.

A Pennsylvania bank barn at the Daniel Boone Homestead, the pioneer's boyhood home.

South of town is a cluster of historic sites, including the **Daniel Boone Homestead** near Birdsboro, childhood home of the legendary pioneer. Although Boone is famous for blazing a trail into Kentucky, he spent his formative years, 1734–50, in a log cabin at this site when Berks County was still on the frontier. The two-story stone house that now stands here was actually built in 1750, the same year that the Boone family moved to North Carolina. A collection of other historic buildings are preserved at the site, including a blacksmith shop, stone smokehouse, log cabin and bank barn, most built after Boone's departure.

Toys are the focus at **Merritt's Museum of Childhood** and **Mary Merritt Doll Museum** about five minutes away in Douglassville. The two museums are packed with some 1,500 dolls, many dating to the Colonial period, as well as model trains, piggy banks, baby carriages, doll houses and an assortment of Indian artifacts and fraktur, the ornate calligraphy of the Pennsylvania Germans.

Costumed interpreters recreate 19th-century life at Hopewell Furnace.

The history of one of the area's many "iron plantations" comes to life a few miles away at **Hopewell Furnace National Historic Site** near Elverston. Built in 1771, Hopewell manufactured a variety of products, including stoves and cookware as well as some of the cannon used by the Continental Army in the Revolutionary War. At its peak, the furnace could consume six tons of raw material – ore, wood, limestone and water – and produce nearly three tons of molten iron in a single day. And when it was "in blast," it lit up the sky for miles around.

The business flickered out in 1883 after decades of decline, but much of the surrounding village remains, including the ironmaster's mansion, schoolhouse, blacksmith shop and the furnace itself. Costumed interpreters help bring the community back to life in summer, demonstrating 19th-century skills like weaving, candlestick making, open-hearth cooking and iron casting. The site is almost completely surrounded by the lovely wooded vales of **French Creek State Park**, with lakes, camping and miles of hiking trails.

You'll find a few attractions scattered in the countryside north of Reading, too, where the hills rise sharply toward the Blue Mountains, an offshoot of the Appalachians. The big event in these parts is the **Kutztown Pennsylvania German Festival**, held in late June and early July. More than 100,000 people pour into the Kutztown Fairgrounds for nine days of folk music, square dancing and traditional crafts like hex-sign painting, quilting, glassblowing and the making of fraktur. There are livestock competitions, antique shows, historic reenactments and, of course, a bounty of rib-sticking Pennsylvania Dutch food. While you're in town, you may also want to hop aboard the vintage diesel-powered trains operated by **East Penn Rail Excursions**. One-hour weekend rides depart from the restored depot just off Main Street and follow the route of the former Allentown and Auburn Railroad.

There are two significant natural sites in the area, too. About four miles northwest of Kutztown is **Crystal Cave**, a maze of subterranean passages eroded from the bedrock over hundreds of thousands of years and still in the process of being formed. Guided tours last about 45 minutes and include an informative video presentation; special candlelight tours are offered on November weekends, recalling the days when the cave was discovered more than 100 years ago.

Farther north is **Hawk Mountain Sanctuary**, a 2,380-acre refuge for eagles, falcons, hawks and other birds of prey that migrate along the Kittatinny Ridge between August and early December. Trails lead from the visitor center to the viewing areas. The highest, North Lookout, is perched atop a rocky 1,521-foot-high promontory about a mile away. The visitor center features a bookstore, art gallery, wildlife viewing area, and museum focusing on the natural history of raptors. An adjacent garden has more than 250 species of flowers, shrubs and trees native to the Appalachian region. Ask about guided walks, demonstrations, lectures and other special programs.

Where to Stay

☆ Adrienne's Inn at Centre Park
730 Centre Avenue, Reading, PA 19601. Tel: 610-374-8557.

Victorian design at its most extravagant is what you'll find at this 18-room stone mansion in the heart of Reading's once-fashionable Centre Park district. Built in the mid-1870s and gloriously refashioned in 1886 by wealthy paint manufacturer Charles Wilhelm, the house is a treasure of architectural details, with hand-carved oak and chestnut woodwork, plaster cherubs, Greek figurines, art glass, period furnishings and more. The two-room Master Suite is the most majestic of the three accommodations. Guests enter a grand study wrapped in chestnut paneling and dominated by an enormous red marble fireplace. The bedroom features a king-sized French Provincial sleigh bed and ornate leaded-glass doors. The Green Room has a softer look, with an elaborate columned stained-glass archway, a bay window with lace curtains and pretty little table-for-two, and tones of cream and muted green. All rooms have 16-foot ceilings, lustrous hardwood floors, and large bathrooms with old-fashioned tiles, fixtures (including, in one room, the first shower head in Reading) and giant claw-foot tubs. Breakfast is served in a sunny room filled with greenery on the first floor; choices include scrambled eggs with red roasted potatoes, pancakes with sausage, and French toast with fresh fruit, among other dishes. Inquire about dinner in one of the glorious dining rooms. Caterers are on hand to prepare whatever you wish. *Rates: $130–$190 double occupancy. Children are welcome with advance notice; no pets. Amenities: three rooms with private bath, air conditioning and cable television, two with fireplace. Porch, garden, parking. AE, MC, V.*

Hampton Inn
1800 Papermill Road, Wyomissing, PA 19610. Tel: 610-374-8100 or toll-free 800-426-7866.

A modern five-story chain hotel near several large shopping complexes just outside of Reading. A good choice for business travelers or families looking for a large, well-kept facility. *Rates: $70–$98 double occupancy. Children are welcome; no pets. Amenities: 125 rooms with private bath, air conditioning and cable television. Free continental breakfast, fitness room, business center, meeting rooms, parking. All major credit cards.*

Hawk Mountain Inn
221 Stony Run Valley Road, Kempton, PA 19529. Tel: 610-756-4224.

Nestled in a pretty little valley across the road from Stony Run Creek about eight miles from Hawk Mountain Sanctuary, this bed-and-breakfast offers eight comfortable rooms furnished simply with a combination of antiques and contemporary pieces, including a few impressive four-poster beds. Each room has a private entrance and a color television tucked into an armoire. Two have a fireplace and two-person Jacuzzi. A full country breakfast – usually whole-wheat pancakes, waffles or eggs, with smoked bacon, fresh fruit and baked goods – is served at two tables by a stone hearth in the great room, where guests can help themselves to snacks, coffee, tea and the built-in beer tap. Tours of Hawk Mountain can be arranged in cooperation with the sanctuary's staff. *Rates: $100–$140 double occupancy. Two-night minimum on holiday weekends and weekends in September and October. Children are welcome; inquire in advance about pets. Amenities: eight rooms with private bath, air conditioning and television, two with fireplace and Jacuzzi. Pool, pond, patio, garden, parking. AE, Dis, MC, V.*

Longswamp Bed and Breakfast

1605 State Street, Mertztown, PA 19539. Tel: 610-682-6197. Fax: 610-682-4854.

Five acres of gardens, orchards and lawn plus another forty acres of forest surround this 18th-century house nestled in the bucolic heart of Berks County about 20 minutes from Reading. Guests are welcome to lounge in a large inviting living room, with light wood floors, fireplace and a generous collection of books and music. Bedrooms in the main house are quite spacious; all have wood floors, recessed windows, lots of healthy plants and a few country antiques. Rachel's Room, which has a metal four-poster bed and cheery floral wallpaper, is particularly pretty. A cottage across the patio from the house affords a bit more seclusion. The building served as a post office in the early 19th century and was later a "station" on the underground railroad. It now contains a snug hideaway

and a two-room suite, both with fireplace. There's a large suite in the cavernous old barn, too. Breakfast is served fireside at one or two tables in the main house. The menu changes from season to season but may include a few favorites like pumpkin waffles, frittatas, bread pudding and blueberry pancakes prepared with homegrown fruits, herbs and vegetables. *Rates: $83–$88 double occupancy. Children are welcome with advance notice; no pets. Amenities: Ten rooms with air conditioning, six with private bath, some with fireplace and/or television. Second-story porch, patio, garden, bicycles, bocce and horseshoe court, parking. AE, MC, V.*

C A M P I N G

Robin Hill Camping Resort

149 Robin Hill Road, Lenhartsville, PA 19534. Tel: 610-756-6117.

Primitive sites, cabins and full hookups, with playground, pool, lake and grocery store on 41 acres.

Where to Eat

Austin's

1101 Snyder Road, Reading, PA 19609. Tel: 610-678-5500.

"Meat so tender it falls off the bone" is no exaggeration when it comes to the baby back ribs at

★ indicates a personal favorite of the author

this popular eatery. They're slow roasted for eight hours before hitting the grill and being slathered with a tangy sauce which, like everything else here, is made from scratch every day. Ribs are only one of the specialties prepared in the open kitchen. Other entrees like aged prime rib, barbecued chicken, and grilled salmon are equally satisfying. Creative pasta includes linguini with grilled shrimp, sun-dried tomatoes, baby spinach and pine nuts, and penne with grilled eggplant, mushrooms and peppers in spicy pomodoro sauce. A lively elevated bar is a popular meeting place. *Moderate. Sun–Thu 11am–9pm, Fri–Sat 11am–10pm. Bar and wine list. No reservations. AE, MC, V.*

Bowers Hotel
Bowers and Old Bowers Road, Bowers, PA 19511.
Tel: 610-682-2900.

To experience the charm of this 19th-century country inn, walk into the gaslit barroom, drop a quarter into the nickelodeon, then move on to a lovely Williamsburg-inspired dining room decorated with paintings by several local artists. An appetizer combo of spinach balls, mushroom caps with sausage stuffing and spare ribs, or Chef Tamara's first-rate chili paves the way for such entrees as seafood Newburg, Dijon chicken strudel, veal Marsala and roast pork loin with fresh cherry salsa. Specials include ethnic dishes like steak fajitas, and crab-and-spinach burritos with jalapeño cheese sauce. Stellar desserts like coffee-toffee crunch torte and bananas Foster cheesecake round out your meal. *Moderate. Lunch Tue–*

Sat noon–3pm; dinner 4pm–9pm, Sun noon–8pm. Bar and wine list. Reservations recommended. AE, Dis, MC, V.

★ Cafe Unicorn
116 Lafayette Street, Hyde Park, Reading, PA 19606.
Tel: 610-929-9992.

Soft music, candlelight, original art and a profusion of fresh flowers set the stage for a romantic evening at this charming hideaway. Peruse the martini menu in an intimate Art Deco lounge while nibbling on complimentary appetizers like crostini topped with salmon mousse. Begin your meal with oysters in champagne sauce, crunchy sesame asparagus spears, or lobster ravioli swimming in caviar cream sauce. Chef James Lesniak's signature dish – charbroiled ostrich steak with cracked pepper, sundried cherries and merlot demiglaze – can be enjoyed as an appetizer or entree. Equally popular is his almond-crusted Dover sole in parsley butter sauce, and oven-roasted rosemary rack of lamb in Bordelaise sauce with brown butter spaetzle. Desserts dazzle; try pear-frangipane tart, Nocello crème brulee, or profiteroles with caramel ice cream and warm chocolate sauce. *Expensive. Dinner Tue–Sat 5pm–9pm. Bar and wine list. Reservations recommended. AE, MC, V.*

Canal Street Pub and Restaurant
535 Canal Street, Reading, PA 19602. Tel: 610-376-4009.

Customers can choose between casual dining in a multilevel pub (with intimate seating in a converted elevator shaft) or a contemporary candlelit dining room where tables are topped with white linen and bottles of garlic and herb-infused olive oil. The in-house Neversink Brewery makes about a dozen beers, many incorporated into dishes like mussels steamed in Kolsch ale and beer-battered mushrooms stuffed with herb cream cheese, both served in the pub. Fancier fare is served in the dining room. The menu changes seasonally but may include pecan-crusted lamb, cioppino, honey Merlot pork, and grilled duck breast in citrus barbecue sauce. Live music on weekends adds to the cheerful din. *Moderate–expensive. Lunch Mon–Sat 11am–2:30pm; dinner Mon–Sat 5pm–10pm. Bar and wine list. Reservations recommended. AE, MC, V.*

✫ Dans'
1049 Penn Street, Reading, PA 19601. Tel: 610-373-2075.

Tin ceilings, tile floors, classical pillars and lavish floral arrangements set the stage for contemporary cuisine at this stylish hideaway. Starters like grilled sea scallops with hazelnut and white bean puree, or baked tortilla with lump crab and Boursin cheese pave the way for such savory entrees as creamy risotto with roasted corn, shiitake mushrooms and arugula, baked pork loin with a stuffing of spinach, porcini mushrooms and pine nuts, or grilled chicken breast and eggplant with yucca puree and Mandarin orange watercress vinaigrette. Desserts are sublime; don't miss the strawberry chantilly. *Moderate–expensive. Lunch Tue–Fri 11:30am–1pm; dinner Tue–Sat 5pm–9pm. Bar and wine list. Reservations recommended. All major credit cards.*

David Stein's Firehouse
Second and Penn Streets, Reading, PA 19602. Tel: 610-374-6222.

The fun starts at this restored 1886 firehouse with a cool collection of firefighting memorabilia – banners, ladders, antique fire helmets, uniforms, the original fire pole and more. A quirky, descriptive menu lists a tantalizing variety of dishes prepared in the open kitchen. Start with appetizers such as Louisiana crab cream soup, chunky beef chili in

a cornbread bowl, or aromatic stuffed mushrooms with warm bread sticks. Entrees run the gamut from Kobe beef and chicken Alfredo to grilled swordfish and pork cutlets over corn and onion salsa. Hot wings, deep-dish pizza and sirloin burgers round out the menu. And don't forget to save room for the tasty apple and cheese pie. Thirteen televisions, a bar with 24 beer taps, and live blues (Fri–Sat night) are good reasons to linger after dinner. *Moderate. Sun–Thu 11am–10pm, Fri–Sat 11am–midnight. Bar and wine list. Reservations recommended. AE, Dis, MC, V.*

Dreamers Cafe
643 Penn Avenue, West Reading, PA 19611. Tel: 610-478-9226.
This multilevel gallery/restaurant stimulates all five senses. The aroma of fresh coffee and croissants infuses the skylit, three-room gallery where local artists show paintings, sculpture, pottery, jewelry and one-of-a-kind installations. When you're done browsing, have a seat next to the free-form fireplace decorated with a profusion of fresh flowers and greenery or perhaps find a sunny spot on the deck out back. Artfully prepared edibles are served on the owner's unique collection of plates – shrimp or melon wrapped in prosciutto with honey-mustard dipping sauce, broiled crab balls with lemon basil dressing, layered tortas with, perhaps, feta, ricotta, cream cheese, bell peppers and pignoli, fresh fruit with Kahlua dip, a variety of flavorful soups, salads, sandwiches and other light fare. Desserts really shine. Key lime pie, pineapple upside-down squares, fruit turnovers and sticky buns only scratch the surface. Live music helps create a mellow mood on weekends. *Budget. Tue–Thu 8am–8pm, Fri–Sat 8am–10pm, Sun 8am–5pm. BYOB. Reservations accepted. AE, MC, V.*

Courtesy of Berks County Visitors Bureau

Dreibelbis Covered Bridge, built in 1869, spans Maiden Creek near Lenhartsville.

Joe's Bistro 614
614 Penn Avenue, West Reading, PA 19611. Tel: 610-371-9966.

Lovers of exotic mushrooms will be tickled by the many fungi-based specialties at this smart bistro about a block from the Vanity Fair outlet complex. Start with the wild mushroom soup, three-mushroom tart or grilled exotic mushrooms on spring greens. Among the entrees, filet mignon en croute with wild mushroom duxelles is a consistent winner, as is a vegetarian mushroom dish known as a portobello pizza. There are several non-mushroom dishes, too, including a full-bodied lamb stew and a good shrimp and mussel dish with saffron sauce over angel-hair pasta. Smashing desserts like a seven-layer butter rum mocha torte or chocolate cabernet tart shouldn't be missed. Fine wines, expert service, and a sunny Mediterranean atmosphere enhance the experience. *Moderate. Lunch Tue–Sat 11:30am–2:30pm; dinner Tue–Sat 5pm–9pm. Bar and wine list. Reservations recommended Fri–Sat. All major credit cards.*

☆ Peanut Bar and Restaurant
332 Penn Street, Reading, PA 19602. Tel: 610-376-8500 or toll-free 800-515-8500.

Family-owned for more than 70 years, this spirited eatery serves up free bowls of peanuts and invites you to toss the shells on the floor. The menu ranges from burgers, soups and salads to more ambitious fare like lump Maryland crab cakes and grilled swordfish osso bucco. It's not unusual to find customers lined up for seasonal specialties like pan-sauteed soft shell crabs doused in pecan brown butter. For lunch, try the blue-plate special, catch of the day or an over-stuffed deli sandwich. Frozen chocolate-covered pretzel pie, vanilla bean crème brulee, apple crisp with homemade cinnamon ice cream and other desserts will weaken the will of the most disciplined dieter. The bar features a wide variety of draft, imported and microbrews, and wines by the glass. *Moderate. Mon–Thu 11am–midnight, Fri–Sat 11am–1am. Bar and wine list. Reservations recommended. AE, Dis, MC, V.*

Stokesay Castle
Hill Road and Spook Lane, Reading, PA 19606. Tel: 610-375-4588.

Situated on ten landscaped acres overlooking the city, this replica of a 13th-century English castle has hand-hewn beams, bas-relief figures, leaded windows, stone columns and suits of armor. Meals are served in several settings – a handsome library with carved oak paneling, the cavernous Great Hall, the Keep Tavern wine cellar, or a flagstone patio with sweeping views. Traditional fare like steak Diane, roast duckling and shrimp Wellington may be served on a hot plank surrounded by veggies and potatoes. Entrees include Stokesay's date-nut pumpkin bread. For dessert, try peach Melba or cherries jubilee, flambeed at your table. Hot and cold sandwiches, soups, salads and other light bites are offered at lunch. *Moderate–expensive. Lunch daily 11:30am–2pm; dinner daily 11:30am–10pm. Bar and wine list. Reservations recommended. All major credit cards.*

What to Do

Berks County Heritage Center
2201 Tulpehocken Road,
Wyomissing, PA 19610.
Tel: 610-374-8839.

You'll find two interesting museums here. Listed on the National Register of Historic Places, the **Gruber Wagon Works** is an intact 19th-century wagon factory. The **C. Howard Hiester Canal Center** displays artifacts and memorabilia from the heyday of Pennsylvania's canal system. A short section of the **Union Canal** passes nearby, crossed by **Wertz's Covered Bridge.** *May–Oct Tue–Sat 10am– 4pm, Sun noon–5pm. Admission to both museums: $5 adults, $4 seniors, $3 students (age 7–18).*

Boyertown Museum of Historic Vehicles
28 Warwick Street, Boyertown,
PA 19512. Tel: 610-367-2090.

Exhibits trace the history of transportation from vintage wagons, bicycles and steam-powered trains to modern automobiles. *Tue–Fri 9am–4pm, Sat–Sun 9:30am–4pm. $4 adults, $3.50 seniors, $2 students (age 6–18).*

Crystal Cave
RD 3, Kutztown, PA 19530.
Tel: 610-683-6765.

A 45-minute walking tour outlines the geology and human history of the cave, gradually carved out of limestone by water over thousands of years. Ask about November candlelight tours. *Mar–Nov daily 9am–5pm, extended summer and holiday hours. $8 adults, $4.75 children (age 4–11).*

Daniel Boone Homestead
400 Daniel Boone Road, Birdsboro,
PA 19508. Tel: 610-582-4900.

Listed in the National Register of Historic Places, the birthplace of Daniel Boone is now home to several historic buildings, including an 18th-century log cabin, Pennsylvania bank barn, blacksmith shop and sawmill. *Tue–Sat 9am–5pm (tours hourly 10am– 4pm), Sun noon–5pm (tours hourly 1pm–4pm); call ahead in winter. Tour $4 adults, $2 children (age 6–12), $3.50 seniors.*

East Penn Rail Excursions/ Kutztown Scenic Train Ride
Railroad Street, P.O. Box 148,
Kutztown, PA 19530.
Tel: 610-683-9202.

Vintage diesel trains depart from historic Kutztown station on an eight-mile, one-hour round-trip along the former route of the Allentown & Auburn Railroad. *Sat–Sun May–Dec; call for departure times and special events.*

Hawk Mountain Sanctuary
1700 Hawk Mountain Road,
Kempton, PA 19529.
Tel: 610-756-6961.

A 2,380-acre refuge dedicated to the preservation of birds of prey, with trails, environmental education programs and visitor center. About 17,000 raptors – hawks, eagles, falcons and others – are sighted here during the migration season, late August to mid-December. *Trails open daily* *dawn–dusk; visitor center daily 9am–5pm, extended hours during migration season. $4 adults, $4 children (age 6–12), $3 seniors.*

Historic Society of Berks County

940 Centre Avenue, Reading, PA 19601. Tel: 610-375-4375.

A collection of historic artifacts and memorabilia. *Tue–Sat 9am–4pm. $2.50 adults, $1 children (age 5–12).*

Hopewell Furnace National Historic Site

2 Mark Bird Lane, Elverson, PA 19520. Tel: 610-582-8773.

A restored "iron plantation," including a waterwheel, barn, schoolhouse, blacksmith shop and ironmaster's mansion as well as a modern visitor center. *Daily 9am–5pm. $4 adults, children free.*

Merritt's Museum of Childhood/ Mary Merritt Doll Museum

907 Benjamin Franklin Highway West, Douglassville, PA 19518. Tel: 610-385-3408 or 610-385-3809.

Both museums are dedicated to antique toys, from lavish Victorian dolls and doll houses to model trains and baby carriages. There's an assortment of other historic objects, too, including fraktur, furniture and American Indian artifacts. *Mon–Sat 10am–4:30pm, Sun 1pm–4:30pm. $3 adults, $1.50 children (age 5–12), $2.50 seniors.*

Mid Atlantic Air Museum

Reading Airport, 11 Museum Drive, Reading, PA 19605. Tel: 610-372-7333.

About 25 vintage aircraft are displayed at this hangar, which includes a restoration shop where planes are returned to fly-ing condition. *Daily 9:30–4pm. $5 adults, $1 children (age 6–12).*

The Pagoda

Skyline Drive, Reading, PA 19601. Tel: 610-655-6374.

Built in 1908 and said to be the only Japanese pagoda east of California, this seven-story structure atop Mount Penn offers panoramic views from the observation deck. *Daily 11am–5pm. Free admission.*

Rodale Institute Experimental Farm

611 Siegfriedale Road, Kutztown, PA 19530. Tel: 610-683-1400.

This 333-acre organic farm offers tours, educational programs, weekly workshops, a bookstore and cafe. *Bookstore daily 9am–5pm; tours May–Oct 15. Inquire about fee for guided tours and programs.*

SHOPPING

Home Furnishings Factory Outlet

Route 10, Morgantown, PA 19543. Tel: 800-226-8011.

An outlet mall specializing in furniture and housewares with such major names as Drexel Hill, Flexsteel, Carolina Classics and many other shops. *Mon–Thu 10am–7pm, Fri–Sat 10am–9pm, Sun noon–5pm.*

Outlets On Hiesters Lane

755 Hiesters Lane, Reading, PA 19604. Tel: 610-921-9394.

Four large stores with discounts on children's clothes and furniture, linens and outerware. *Mon–Sat 9:30am–9pm, Sun 10am–5pm.*

Designers Place at VF Outlet Village specializes in brand-name fashions.

Reading Outlet Center
801 North Ninth Street, Reading, PA 19604. Tel: 610-373-5495.

More than 70 outlets featuring well-known brand names like Levi's, Ralph Lauren, Calvin Klein, Tommy Hilfiger, J. Crew and many more. *Mon–Sat 9:30am–8pm, Sun 10am–6pm.*

Reading Station Outlets
951 North Sixth Street, Reading, PA 19601. Tel: 610-478-7000.

Brooks Brothers, Nine West, Allen Edmonds are just a few of the designers you'll find at this complex of 25 fashion outlets. *Mon–Thu 10am–7pm, Fri–Sat 10am–8pm, Sun 11am–5pm.*

**Renninger's Antique
and Flea Market**
740 Noble Street, Kutztown, PA
19530. Tel: 610-385-0104.

A sprawling antique and farmers'
market with scores of vendors
at indoor and outdoor stalls.
*Antique market Sat 8am–4pm.
Farmers' market Fri 10am–7pm,
Sat 8am–4pm.*

VF Outlet Village
Penn Avenue and Park Road, West
Reading, PA 19610. Tel: 610-378-0408
or toll-free 800-772-8336.

The biggest complex in the
Reading area, with more than 90
outlets, from Anne Klein, Liz
Claiborne and London Fog to
Reebok and Black & Decker.
*Mon–Thu, Sat 9am–7pm, Fri
9am–9pm, Sun 10am–5pm.*

SPECIAL EVENTS

June
**Fiddle and Acoustic Music
Mini Fest**
Berks County Heritage Center,
2201 Tulpehocken Road,
Wyomissing, PA 19610.
Tel: 610-374-8839.

Hear some of the region's best
country, folk and bluegrass
musicians at this daylong
outdoor festival.

June–July
**Kutztown Pennsylvania
German Festival**
Kutztown Fairgrounds, Kutztown,
PA 19530. Tel: 800-963-8824.

One of the area's premier events,
the festival celebrates Pennsylvania Dutch culture with demonstrations of such traditional
activities as hex-sign painting,
quilting, fraktur, dancing and
sheepshearing as well as live-

stock and produce competitions,
bake-offs, games, rides and plenty of Pennsylvania German food.

August
Annual GardenFest
Rodale Institute Experimental Farm,
Siegfriedale Road, Kutztown, PA
19530. Tel: 610-683-1400.

A daylong event focusing on
organic gardening and sustain-
able agriculture, with a variety
of children's programs, a choice
of some 50 seminars and workshops, select craftspeople, an art
exhibit, farm market and food
court.

September
Apple Harvest Day
Hopewell Furnace National Historic
Site, 2 Mark Bird Lane, Elverson,
PA 19520. Tel: 610-582-8773.

Experience harvest time in the
19th century as costumed craftspeople and rangers recreate life
at this "iron plantation" in the
1830s.

**Arts and Antiques Fair in
Centre Park**
Centre Park, Reading, PA.
Tel: 610-375-7860.

An outdoor fair and sale in the
Centre Park Historic District.

INFORMATION

**Reading and Berks County
Visitors Bureau**
VF Factory Outlet, Park Road and
Hill Avenue, P.O. Box 6677, Reading,
PA 19610. Tel: 610-375-4085 or
toll-free 800-443-6610.

HIGHLIGHTS

- Mount Gretna
- Cornwall Iron Furnace
- Lebanon County Historical Society and the Stoy Museum
- Union Canal Tunnel Park

Lebanon County

*I*n 1797, George Washington sent his servant to Lebanon with $25 to see the famed minister and physician William Henry Stoy, who reportedly had a cure for rabies. The prescription? "One ounce of herb, red chickweed, four ounces of theriac, and one quart of beer, all well digested, the dose being a wine glass full."

How Dr. Stoy came up with that remedy is anybody's guess, but at least one volume of county history suggests that it may have succeeded only because most of the animals weren't really rabid after all. Not surprisingly, Stoy is no longer celebrated for his rabies "cure" or any other medical breakthroughs, but he is one of dozens of figures who hold a special place in county history.

Lebanon Valley was first settled in 1732 by refugees from the Palatinate region of Germany who came seeking religious freedom. They found a land of fertile soil and winding creeks that was perfectly suited to their agrarian way of life.

Today, the valley remains a peaceful, rural oasis dotted with pretty farmhouses, produce stands and a patchwork of fields and meadows. Much of tradition-al German culture persists

A cottage nestled in the woods of Mount Gretna. Right, roadside stands offer a bounty of fresh fruits and vegetables.

as well, from colorful hex signs and folk art to the locally-made bologna, a spicier, smokier concoction than the pasty pink stuff you find at the supermarket.

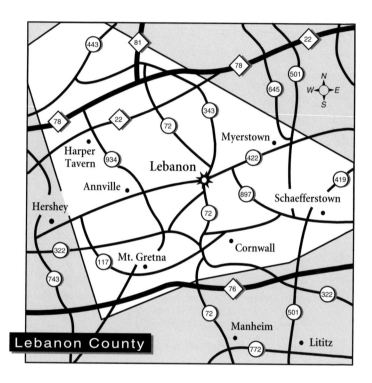

Perhaps the best place to start exploring is at the former home of the illustrious Dr. Stoy, an 18th-century Georgian mansion in downtown Lebanon that now houses the **Lebanon County Historical Society** and **Stoy Museum**. The mansion also served as the county courthouse for a few years in the early 1800s. In fact, a young attorney by the name of James Buchanan made his legal debut here in 1813. He later became the county's first district attorney and, of course, the 15th President of the United States. Allow at least two hours to enjoy a guided tour of the museum.

The items on display span more than two centuries. Some are historically significant, others are just outdated and fun to look at. A few of the museum's treasures include a jersey that Babe Ruth wore in 1918 when he played for Lebanon's Bethlehem Steel baseball team to avoid the military draft; a loving cup that former President Theodore Roosevelt sent to the nearby village of Bismarck when it changed its name to Quentin in honor of his son, Quentin, killed in World War I; a horrific-looking contraption used to curl women's hair; and a massive 1774 pumper wagon, the third oldest fire apparatus in the state.

Down in the basement, near the end of your tour, you'll find an unassuming little safe once used in the office of the Union Canal. The safe itself is unremarkable, but the canal is another story.

Completed in 1828, the canal ran 82 miles between the Susquehanna River and Schuylkill River from Reading to Middletown. The waterway was plagued with problems from the very beginning – poorly designed locks, floods, costly repairs and, later, competition with the railroads. It finally went out of business in 1885 without ever realizing its potential.

Today, the only navigable section of the canal is a third-of-a-mile stretch just outside of town at the **Union Canal Tunnel Park**, which also features one of the oldest tunnels in the United States. Originally 729 feet long, the Union Canal Tunnel was drilled by hand and blasted with gunpowder at a grueling rate of 15 linear feet per week. You can stroll to the tunnel on a shaded towpath or, if you're lucky, go the way that 19th-century canal-

Gothic window and thick sandstone wall at historic Cornwall Iron Furnace.

men went – on a mule-drawn barge. Your guide may even pause to let you pick sweet summer cherries from branches hanging over the canal.

The park is open year-round, but volunteer shortages have limited public barge rides to three days a year: the two-day **Union Canal Days** festival in May and an old-fashioned community picnic in late September. School or community groups can arrange special rides throughout the year, and if you happen to be visiting, they'll be glad to take you along.

You'll find another important piece of history just south of town at the **Cornwall Iron Furnace**, the most well-preserved of its kind in the Western Hemisphere. And with its beautiful red sandstone buildings and gothic revival windows, it's a celebration of form as well as function.

Peter Grubb built the furnace in 1742 and named it Cornwall in honor of the English county where his father was born. With the valley's rich supply of limestone, iron ore and timber – all basic ingredients in the production of iron – the "iron planta-tion" thrived well into the 19th century. During the Revolutionary War, it produced 42 cannon, ammunition and other equipment for George Washington's army.

Try to avoid touring the facility on a sweltering day. Some places are downright stifling, although it's nothing like the 160-

Cornwall Iron Furnace produced cannon and ammunition for the Continental Army.

degree temperatures that workers endured in the cast house when the furnace was tapping. At the center of the operation is the furnace's awesome 30-foot stack, where temperatures soared to the 3,000 degrees needed to melt iron. Pay special attention to the steam engine that powered a massive 24-foot wheel used to pump air into the furnace.

The furnace closed in 1883, due largely to the development of the anthracite coal industry. However, mining in the area continued for almost another century. Walk a short distance past the furnace and you'll find yourself at the **Cornwall Ore Banks**, once the largest open mining pit in the East. In 1972, after two centuries of mining had gradually depleted resources, Hurricane Agnes dealt the final blow. Today, the water level in the abandoned pit stands at about 450 feet.

Just a short walk down the road is **Minersvillage**, so named because it served as home to employees of the ore banks. Minersvillage is but a single street, reminiscent of something you might find in the English countryside, with snug stone cottages, now privately owned.

If the ways of a bygone era are all but a distant memory in Cornwall, they are alive and well in nearby **Mount Gretna**, which was once considered part of the iron plantation. It's not the blast of the iron furnace that keeps this community thriving; it's the sound of music, the lure of the stage, and simple faith.

Tucked into the **Furnace Hills** a few short miles south of Cornwall, Mount Gretna was born in 1882 as a station along the Cornwall and Lebanon Railroad. Railroad president Robert Coleman and others soon saw its value as a picnic spot and recreation area. In the ensuing years, they built a dam across Conewago Creek to form a lake, laid a dance floor, installed a carousel, and built a luxury hotel.

In 1891, two areas of cottages were built at Mount Gretna – the Campmeeting Grounds and the Chautauqua. The former accommodated the summer religious meetings of the United Brethren Church. The latter was modeled after the original Chautauqua in New York, an educational movement for the advancement of literary and scientific knowledge.

The hotel, dance floor and merry-go-round are gone now, but the beautiful scenery and community philosophy remain. Mount Gretna lies rather dormant in winter, but once the summer season opens it's alive with activity. Religious camp meetings are held for several weeks, and the **Gretna Playhouse** offers a full slate of plays and musicals featuring talent from this region and beyond. A young Charlton Heston honed his acting skills here in the 1940s. There are daily craft and educational programs, weekend concerts with everything from chamber music to bluegrass and jazz, even weekly book reviews. Stop by on a summer weekend and you'll find folks headed to a performance at the playhouse, enjoying a heaping glass of ice cream at the always-packed Jigger Shop, or strolling the maze of narrow streets crowded with charming Victorian cottages.

Mount Gretna has long been known as a center of the arts, attracting actors, craftsmen and musicians.

Where to Stay

Hen-Apple Bed and Breakfast
409 South Lingle Avenue, Palmyra, PA 17078. Tel: 717-838-8282.

You'll find country charm in every corner of this deceptively large farmhouse, built by a German yeoman about 1825 with a spacious modern addition. The generous common rooms set the folksy tone of the place. Two parlors – one with red-checkered armchairs and sofa, the other with wicker furniture – are filled with quilts, hanging baskets, wall stencils and other quaint colorful details. The theme continues in the two fanciest accommodations – the Forest Shade and Rose rooms – both rather snug but prettily furnished with an assortment of antique chests and bureaus, lace curtains, wood floors and oriental or braided rugs. The Forest Shade Room has a lovely crocheted canopy bed. There are four additional rooms up the back staircase, two of which – the Amish and Mallard rooms – are quite large and somewhat more contemporary in style. A full country breakfast often features stuffed French toast with rum raisin sauce or egg casserole with herb biscuits, served in one of two dining rooms or on the veranda. *Rates: $75 double occupancy. Two–night minimum on select holidays. No children or pets. Amenities: Six rooms with private bath and air conditioning. Veranda, garden, parking. AE, Dis, MC, V.*

Mount Gretna Inn
Kauffman and Pine, Mount Gretna, PA 17064. Tel: 717-964-3234 or toll-free 800-277-6602. Fax: 717-964-3641.

Built in 1921 by Abraham Lincoln Kauffman, one of the entrepreneurs behind the development of Mount Gretna, this stucco arts-and-crafts inn was at one time a popular hangout for actors who appeared at the nearby playhouse. It's said that a young Charlton Heston was tossed out of the bar in the 1940s. Today, the inn offers eight homey guest rooms. The largest and most comfortably furnished are the Wild Cherry and Chestnut Suite, both with wood floors, queen beds, carved headboards, a few antiques and sunny sitting areas. Common rooms include a spacious living room with patterned wood floor, stone fireplace and baby-grand piano. Breakfast changes daily but may include stuffed French toast with hot raspberry syrup or egg and cheese angel puffs, all served at three large tables in the dining room. Breakfast is also offered in the Chestnut Suite upon request. Guests are welcome to lounge on the large front porch, perfect for an early cup of tea or late-night drink. The inn is set near 4,000 acres of protected forest with an excellent network of trails. Mountain bike rentals can be arranged by the innkeepers with advance notice. *Rates: $85–$125 double occupancy. Two-night minimum on August and October weekends. Children over 12 are welcome; no pets. Amenities: Eight rooms with private bath (one in corridor) and air conditioning; six rooms with gas fireplace. Porch, garden, parking. AE, Dis, MC, V.*

★ Rexmont Inn

299 Rexmont Road, P.O. Box 127, Rexmont, PA 17085.
Tel: 717-274-2669 or toll-free 800-626-0942. Fax: 717-274-2774.

It's said that a ghost roams this romantic 19th-century inn about a mile from the historic Cornwall Iron Furnace. Some folks believe it's the long-dead niece of the original owner, Cyrus Rex, a wealthy banker and entrepreneur, although one psychic says it's Cyrus himself, indulging in a bit of transvestism. Cross-dressing ghosts aside, the inn boasts seven handsome guest rooms, furnished in a plush but understated period style. The Cyrus Rex and Susan Amanda rooms are the most elegant, with wood floors, high ceilings, ornate carved headboards, marble-top vanities, a velvet settee, leather rocker and other gracious appointments. Downstairs you'll

Blast equipment at Cornwall Iron Furnace.

find a gift shop and lounge where Rex once ran a general store and post office. There's a more formal parlor, too, as well as a sunny "morning coffee" room, filled with wicker furniture, games and greenery. A champagne breakfast is served at several tables-for-two in the dining room and may feature such dishes as heart-shaped waffles with clementine sauce and home-baked coffee cake. Special events at the inn include English high tea (by reservation), live chamber music and talks on herbology in the extensive gardens, as well as the "Mind, Body, Spirit Weekend," featuring massage and meditation techniques, and "A Weekend with a Psychic," with seminars on various New Age topics. Ask about dinner and theater packages, too. *Rates: $95–$105 double occupancy. Children are welcome with advance notice; no pets. Amenities: Seven rooms with private bath and air conditioning. Patio, gardens, gift shop, parking. AE, MC, V.*

Swatara Creek Inn
Jonestown Road, R.D. 2, Box 692, Annville, PA 17003. Tel: 717-865-3259.

Built in 1860 and once owned by chocolate mogul Milton Hershey, who used it to house boys attending his charitable industrial school, this hulking brick Victorian stands on a hillock surrounded by farmland about 20 minutes from Hersheypark. Ten large rooms with 10- or 12-foot ceilings, including a two-room suite, are simply furnished with hefty four-poster canopy beds, quilts, carpet, lace curtains and pretty wallpaper. Some

rooms have additional daybeds. A full breakfast of, say, waffles, French toast or bacon and eggs with fresh fruit, shoofly pie or cookies is served at the gargantuan, 28-person dining-room table, made from a spruce tree that was struck by lightning in the back yard. *Rates: $55–$80 double occupancy. Children are welcome; no pets. One room is wheelchair-accessible. Amenities: Ten rooms with private bath and air conditioning. Gift shop, porch, garden, parking. All major credit cards.*

Where to Eat

Jigger Shop
Route 117, Mount Gretna, PA 17064. Tel: 717-964-9686.

A local institution, this old-fashioned ice-cream parlor is famous for its luscious sundaes and heaping cones. *Budget. May–Sep, call for hours. No credit cards.*

☆ Tony's Mining Company
211 Rexmont Road, Cornwall, PA 17016-0123. Tel: 717-273-4871.

It may look like an old mining shed from the outside, but inside you'll find a truly fine restaurant. Historic photos, heavy timbers and a fascinating collection of mining memorabilia give the interior a rustic atmosphere offset by gleaming copper-topped

☆ indicates a personal favorite of the author

tables and brass candleholders. The menu isn't extensive but is exceptionally well-prepared. Among the appetizers, smoked pheasant sausage in cognac, and broiled clams topped with crab-meat and Hollandaise sauce are consistent winners. Entrees include a savory boneless quail stuffed with sausage, crab and shiitake mushrooms, pork loin crusted with macadamia nuts, blackened yellow fin tuna with a creamy garlic-tomato sauce, and a variety of beef and pasta dishes. *Moderate. Tue–Fri 5:30pm–9pm, Sat 5pm–9:30pm. Bar and wine list. Reservations recommended. AE, Dis, MC, V.*

Trattoria Fratelli
502 East Lehman Street, Lebanon, PA 17046. Tel: 717-273-1443.

Crisp, bubbling, brick-oven pizza is only the beginning at this cozy trattoria. A modest but interesting menu features tradi-tional Italian cuisine with intriguing twists – sage gnocchi with butternut squash and spinach, wild mushroom cannel-loni with grilled duck, eggplant relish and bechamel sauce, and a variety of panini on crusty homemade bread. There's a good choice of antipasti, too, including tangy calamari with red bliss potatoes and sauteed peppers, and a vinaigrette salad of mixed greens, grilled figs, gor-gonzola and walnuts. Exposed beams and brick walls add to the homey atmosphere. Alfresco dining is available in warm weather. Cappuccino and silky gelato finish your meal on an appropriately indulgent note. *Moderate. Tue–Sat 4pm–10pm. Bar and wine list. No reservations. MC, V.*

Maple Street Cafe
801 Maple Street, Lebanon, PA 17046. Tel: 717-272-0597.

Sunlight streams into the tall narrow windows at the front of this casual eatery, housed in an old brick tavern decorated with quilts and collectibles. The kitchen can be trusted to turn out well-done meat and fish dishes, including a tasty crab-meat casserole, tangy seafood crepe, barbecued ribs, and filet tips with burgundy mushroom sauce. Lunch brings a variety of thick sandwiches (try the hot pot roast and gravy or beef and bleu cheese sub), omelettes, burgers and salads, most named after sports teams and figures. The bar is a fun, low-key place to watch a game or hang out with friends. *Moderate. Lunch Tue–Fri 11:30am–2pm, dinner Mon–Sat 5pm–10pm. Bar. Reservations recommended. No credit cards.*

What to Do

ATTRACTIONS

Cornwall Iron Furnace
Rexmont Road at Boyd Street, P.O. Box 251, Cornwall, PA 17016. Tel: 717-272-9711.

A well-preserved 18th-century iron furnace and community, with visitor center and guided tours. *Tue–Sat 10am–4pm, Sun noon–4pm; extended summer* *hours. $3.50 adults, $3 seniors, $1.50 children (age 6–12).*

Gretna Playhouse
P.O. Box 578, Mount Gretna, PA 17064. Tel: 717-964-3370.

Music at Gretna, P.O. Box 519, Mount Gretna, PA 17064. Tel: 717-361-1508.

This open-air theater has been presenting fine theater, music, dance and other performances for more than 70 years. The season runs from June through August. Call for schedule and ticket prices.

Seltzer's-Bomberger's Lebanon Bologna
230 North College Street, Palmyra, PA 17078. Tel: 717-838-6336.

Exhibit and outlet store at one of the area's biggest makers of bologna, prepared with traditional ingredients and hung by hand in wooden smokehouses. *Mon–Fri 7am–5pm, Sat 8am–1pm.*

Stoy Museum and Lebanon County Historical Society
924 Cumberland Street, Lebanon, PA 17042. Tel: 717-272-1473.

A collection of historic artifacts and memorabilia from the Lebanon area. *Tours Sun–Fri 1pm–3pm. $3 adults, $2.50 seniors, $1 children (age 5–12).*

Weaver's Famous–Baum's Lebanon Bologna Company
15th Avenue and Weavertown Road, Lebanon, PA 17042. Tel: 717-274-6100.

An outlet shop and small exhibit on the making of Lebanon's savory smoked meats. *Mon–Sat 9am–4pm. Free admission.*

SPECIAL EVENTS

May
Union Canal Days
Union Canal Tunnel Park

A two-day festival with mule-drawn barge rides, food, crafts and other programs illustrating canal history.

July
Lebanon Fair
County Fairgrounds. Tel: 717-273-3670.

An old-fashioned agricultural fair with livestock contests, entertainment, rides and lots of country-style food and crafts.

August
Mount Gretna Outdoor Art Show
Chautauqua Grounds. Tel: 717-964-2340.

A juried art and craft show, with live music and plenty of food.

September
Schaefferstown Harvest Fair
Schaefferstown Farm Museum. Tel: 717-949-3235.

A celebration of early-American farm life, with horse and oxen demonstrations, hay rides, cider making, threshing, folk art and entertainment.

INFORMATION

Lebanon Valley Tourist and Visitor Bureau
Quality Inn, 6254 Quentin Road, Lebanon, PA 17042. Tel: 717-272-8555.

HIGHLIGHTS

- Hersheypark
- ZooAmerica
- Chocolate World
- Hershey Gardens
- Hershey Museum

Hershey

he guy who put this place on the map was born here in 1857 when the town was a little farming community named Derry Church. Long before he passed on in 1945, he had transformed it into the chocolate-manufacturing empire and recreational hub that now bears his name. Today, his factory churns out 33 million Hershey Kisses a day, zillions of Hershey bars a year, and a raft of other chocolate products.

His name was Milton Snavely Hershey, candy mogul and philanthropist. Raised by Mennonite parents, he left school after the fourth grade, apprenticing first with a printer and then with a Lancaster candymaker. At just 19 he opened his own candy operation in Philadelphia, and in 1903 he built what is still the largest chocolate-making plant in the world, smack in the middle of his native farm country.

Millions come each year to visit the small town of Hershey, Pennsylvania. They see street lights shaped like Hershey Kisses, ride roller coasters at Hersheypark, enjoy ballet and Broadway shows at the palatial Hershey Theatre, and stroll through the manicured grounds of Hershey Gardens.

Founders Hall, Milton Hershey School. Right, a signpost in downtown Hershey, "the sweetest place on Earth."

Hershey opened his first candy operation in Philadelphia in 1876, the year of the big Centennial exhibition. The business quickly went belly up, as did three other attempts in Chicago, Denver and New York. Penniless, he borrowed funds to return home and launch the Lancaster Caramel Company in 1886.

In 1893, at the big Chicago International Exposition, he bought German chocolate-making equipment and soon discovered how to make milk chocolate, cocoa and baking chocolate. Seven years later, Hershey sold his caramel company for $1 million and decided to concentrate exclusively on the manufacture of chocolate. This time he built a factory, not in an urban setting but back home in Derry Church.

Hershey built what is still the largest chocolate-making plant in the world.

Because of health regulations, visitors can no longer tour the plant, but you can view a snazzy reproduction of the chocolate-making process at the **Chocolate World** visitor center near Hersheypark. The free ride takes you from cocoa beans to candy bars with the help of an animated Hershey Kiss. When you disembark, you'll get a free sample and an opportunity to buy hundreds of Hershey products.

Walk off your treats with a three-minute hike to the **Hershey Museum**. Originally built to showcase American Indian culture,

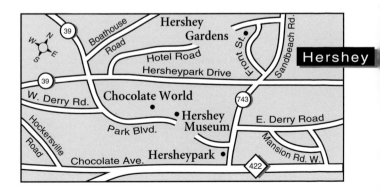

the museum now features much more, including exhibits on the Victorian era and on Pennsylvania Germans. Don't miss the 600-pound, 1,200-piece cut-glass torchiere that once graced the foyer of High Point, the mansion Hershey shared with his wife, Catherine. Another treat is the Monumental Apostolic Clock, built in 1878 by Lancastrian John Fiester and billed as the ninth wonder of the world. A guide will explain the intri-

cate workings of the 12-foot clock, but the real thrill is when it strikes a quarter to the hour and a procession of Apostles moves past Christ. Keep an eye out for the devil; he pops up in three different places. Of course, the Hershey Museum also has an extensive exhibit on Hershey and his town. There are furnishings from High Point, old chocolate-making equipment, and artifacts from the early days of Derry Church.

Most of this model town was built by the candymaker for the people who worked in his factory. He planned the public education system and offered buildings and finances to a variety of civic groups like the library and fire company. He also wanted his employees to enjoy culture and recreation, so he built the **Hershey Theatre** and the now-famous **Hersheypark**, which has grown from a popular picnic spot to a full-fledged amusement park.

Visiting Hersheypark takes a full day. Thrill-seekers can turn their stomachs on roller coasters made of old-fashioned wood or twisting steel. The faint of heart can drive motorized antique cars on a replica of the Pennsylvania Turnpike, get soaking wet at the Canyon River Rapids, take in a dolphin and sea lion show, or listen to live music in the amphitheatre. Be sure to leave time for the

Hersheypark has six roller coasters, from high-speed loop-the-loops to a classic 1920s wooden cyclone.

adjacent **ZooAmerica North American Wildlife Park**, an 11-acre zoo that Hershey opened in the early 1900s to showcase his collection of wild animals. It features more than 75 North American species, from ravens and prairie dogs to elk and bison.

For a relaxing and entertaining overview of other points of interest, take one of the trolley tours that leaves hourly from Chocolate World. Guides dressed in Victorian garb will regale you with Hershey stories, homespun humor and good old-fashioned sing-alongs. If you're not old enough to remember standards like "Sentimental Journey," "A Bicycle Built for Two" and "Bye-Bye Blackbird," don't worry. Song sheets are provided.

The hour-long tour will take you past Hershey's 22-room **High Point** mansion and his birthplace, which his grandfather Isaac built in 1826. Neither is open to the public, but you may be lucky enough to meet Hershey's "reincarnated" mother and father and some other colorful characters from the town's past who conveniently pop onto the bus whenever it comes to a stop. Hershey's "mother" may even pass out a few treats as she recalls how she used to hand-wrap her son's chocolate Kisses when she was well into her 80s.

You'll also see the **Milton Hershey School for Boys** which the childless Hersheys founded in 1909 to provide education and care for orphans. When Catherine Hershey died in 1915, Hershey put $60 million in trust for the school. Today, it's home to 1,200 boys and girls who are either orphaned or have only one parent who is unable to care for them. A focal point of the campus is Founders Hall. Free tours of the building are available, but you'll want to look at it from a distance to admire its unsupported dome, second in size only to the one on St. Peter's Basilica in Rome.

What started as a small community garden now sprawls across 23 manicured acres.

If you appreciate spectacular floral displays, a simple drive past **Hershey Gardens** won't be enough. What started in 1937 as a community rose garden has blossomed into 23 acres with 15,000 roses, themed gardens and an impressive variety of trees like giant sequoia and oriental spruce. Kids and adults will enjoy the new butterfly house – the largest in Pennsylvania – with several hundred colorful butterflies.

A few years before the gardens were planted, Hershey's "Great Building Campaign" of the Great Depression produced a few other landmarks. The **Hotel Hershey**, for instance, was modeled after several Mediterranean palaces, including the Heliopolis in Cairo, Egypt, which the Hersheys once visited. The entire complex sits on a 300-acre hilltop overlooking formal gardens and the amusement park. And the Hershey Theatre, main occupant of the behemoth $3 million Community Center built in 1933, is well worth the price of admission. The grand lobby alone features an Italian lava rock floor, arches made from four different types of marble, and bas-relief images on the ceiling. Performances include Broadway shows, big bands and classical music.

Like so much in Hershey, the theater reflects the elegance of a bygone era. And it's all part of the legacy of a farm boy with a fourth-grade education and, you might say, a sweet disposition.

Aerial view of the Milton Hershey School, founded by the chocolate-maker and his wife in 1909. The school encompasses some 50 farms and 10,000 acres.

Where to Stay

☆ Hotel Hershey

Hotel Road, P.O. Box 400, Hershey, PA 17033-0400. Tel: 717-533-2171. Fax: 717-534-8887.

Built in a whimsical Mediterranean style, this palatial hotel sprawls across 90 acres on a hilltop overlooking manicured gardens. Mosaic floors, splendid art, chandeliers, fountains and reflecting pools are just a few of the grand touches that make the place a hit with convention-goers and, increasingly, families. The rooms vary in configuration and decor, some with traditional European style, others with a toned-down contemporary feeling. Fine cuisine is served at the exceptional Circular Dining Room (see "Where To Eat"). The more casual Fountain Cafe may be a better choice for dinner with the kiddies. *Rates: $178–$258 double occupancy. Children are welcome; no pets. Amenities: 214 rooms with private bath, air conditioning, cable television, sitting area. Extensive banquet and meeting facilities. Two restaurants, cafe, lounge, live entertainment. Extensive garden, nine-hole golf course, tennis courts, indoor and outdoor pools, whirlpool, saunas, exercise room, jogging trails, horseback riding. All major credit cards.*

Hershey Lodge and Convention Center

West Chocolate Avenue and University Drive, Hershey, PA 17033. Tel: 717-533-3311.

A modern and less expensive alternative to the Hotel Hershey is this giant complex, with some 450 rooms, tennis courts, pools, cinema and other recreational facilities. Three restaurants offer plenty of options: the Hearth for homey regional fare, the Hershey Grill for steak and seafood, and Lebbie Lebkicher's for straightforward food and family-friendly atmosphere. *Rates: $118–$178 double occupancy. Children are welcome; no pets. Amenities: 457 rooms with private bath, air conditioning, cable television. Extensive banquet, convention and meeting facilities. Three restaurants, two bars, live entertainment. Golf course, tennis courts, indoor and outdoor pools, whirlpool, saunas, exercise room, bicycles, movie theater. All major credit cards.*

Where to Eat

Al Mediterraneo

288 East Main Street, Hummelstown, PA 17036. Tel: 717-566-5086.

This classy Italian restaurant is located in Hummelstown but is close to all Hershey attractions. Seek romantic seclusion upstairs

☆ indicates a personal favorite of the author

at one of a handful of tables overlooking the main dining room. Or feel the energy mount in the chatty front room downstairs. The menu features robust southern Italian cuisine suffused with fresh herbs and olive oil. Start with gourmet wood-oven pizza, hot antipasti or pasta and white bean soup, and then move on to chicken saltimbocca, veal Marsala, Mediterranean seafood stew or tender lamb chops no bigger than silver dollars, among other specialties. A slice of ethereal white chocolate mousse cake finishes the meal with an indulgent flourish. *Moderate–expensive. Lunch Mon–Fri 11:30am–3pm; dinner Mon–Thu 5pm–10pm, Fri–Sat 5pm–11pm. Bar and wine list. Reservations recommended. Valet parking. AE, Dis, MC, V.*

More than 50,000 tulips and 15,000 roses bloom at Hershey Gardens.

★ Circular Dining Room at the Hershey Hotel

Hotel Road, Hershey, PA 17033-0400. Tel: 717-533-2171.

"In some places if you don't tip well, they put you in a corner," Milton Hershey observed while planning this elegant restaurant. "I don't want any corners." Nobody sits in the corner at this hotel dining room, wrapped with stained-glass windows overlooking manicured gardens. The room is quite spacious, but soothing music, elegant table settings and attentive service lend a touch of intimacy. A typical evening might start with wild mushroom and truffle au gratin, sauteed escargot or rich smoked duck consommé. Stylishly presented entrees feature such dishes as sauteed sea bass with cabbage-salsify confetti, grilled breast of duckling in a pool of pomegranate-mustard jus, and venison en croute with currant tapenade and hazelnut sauce. Desserts like the triple-chocolate-truffle torte, giant chocolate-covered strawberries, and multi-tiered cakes provide a spectacular finish. The lunch buffet and Sunday brunch are equally appealing. *Expensive. Breakfast daily 7am–10am; lunch daily 11:30am–2pm (seatings every 15 minutes); dinner daily 5:30pm–9pm (seatings every 30 minutes); Sunday brunch 11:45am–2pm (seatings at 11:45am, noon, 1:45pm, 2pm). Bar and wine list. Reservations recommended. Jackets required for dinner. Pianist Fri–Sat night and Sun morning. All major credit cards.*

Hershey Grill

Hershey Lodge, West Chocolate Avenue and University Drive, Hershey, PA 17033.
Tel: 717-533-3311.

Eclectic, well-prepared cuisine is the attraction at this casual bistro adjacent to the Hershey Lodge. Most dishes have a straightforward American appeal – thick steaks and burgers, Chesapeake crab chowder, honey bourbon salmon, blackened catfish. But there are several Italian and French dishes, too, including wild mushroom ravioli, fettuccine primavera and grilled chicken Oscar. Calorie-counters can ask for a half-portion of luscious desserts. Dining on the outdoor patio is available on summer evenings. *Moderate. Lunch Mon–Sat 11am–4pm; dinner Mon–Thu 4pm–9pm, Fri–Sat 4pm–10pm, Sun 4:30pm–9pm; Sun brunch 11am–2:30pm. Bar and wine list. Reservations recommended. All major credit cards.*

Restaurant on Chocolate

814 East Chocolate Avenue, Hershey, PA 17033.
Tel: 717-534-2734.

Take a giant leap away from meat and potatoes at this popular upscale eatery about a mile outside of downtown Hershey. The cuisine is American with a few Southwestern touches. Beautifully presented dishes include appetizers like grilled shrimp textured with black and white sesame seeds or green lip mussels and clams over a bed of cappellini. Entrees include pecan-crusted chicken with black bean sauce and grilled tortillas, grilled lamb chops with pink peppercorns, rosemary and Dijon mustard,

and Atlantic salmon with honey, lemon and walnut-herb crust. An extensive wine list features a thoughtful selection of imported and California labels. Leave room for dessert; it's irresistible. *Moderate–expensive. Lunch Mon–Fri 11am–2:30pm; dinner Mon–Sat 5pm–10pm. Bar and wine list. Reservations highly recommended. All major credit cards.*

What to Do

ATTRACTIONS

Chocolate World

800 Park Boulevard, Hershey, PA 17033. Tel: 717-534-4900.

An automated tour of the chocolate-making process from the growing of cocoa to the creation of the "kiss" and traditional candy bar. A shopping complex at the end of the tour offers all sorts of Hershey chocolate and related products. *Daily 9am–4:45pm; hours vary by season, call ahead for schedule. Free admission.*

Hershey Gardens

P.O. Box 416, Hotel Road, Hershey, PA 17033. Tel: 717-534-3493.

More than 20 acres of trees, shrubs and flowers arranged in several theme areas – colonial garden, Japanese garden, English garden, rose garden and more. *Apr–Oct Mon–Thu 9am–6pm, Fri–Sat 9am–8pm. $5 adults,*

$4.50 seniors, $2.50 children (age 3–15).

Hershey Museum
170 West Hershey Park Drive, Hershey, PA 17033.
Tel: 717-534-3439.

A fascinating collection of American Indian and Pennsylvania German artifacts, including early-American furniture, textiles, pottery and folk art; the museum also details the life story of Milton Hershey and the development of his company. *Daily 10am–5pm, extended summer hours. $4.25 adults, $3.75 seniors, $2 children (age 3–15).*

Hersheypark
100 West Hersheypark Drive, Hershey, PA 17033.
Tel: 717-534-3090.

A state-of-the-art amusement park with more than 50 rides, from white-knuckle high-speed roller coasters, water slides, a monorail and Ferris wheel to a charming hand-carved carousel built in 1911. There are recreated German and English villages for shopping, dozens of snack bars and restaurants, and lots of live entertainment. *May–Sep daily; call for hours. $29.95 adults, $16.95 seniors, $16.95 children (age 3–8).*

Hersheypark Arena
Box office: 100 West Hersheypark Drive, P.O. Box 866, Hershey, PA 17033. Tel: 717-534-3911.

The box office handles tickets for events at the 10,000-seat arena, which features big-name entertainers and a minor-league hockey team, the Hershey Bears, as well as Hersheypark Stadium, which has college football and outdoor concerts. *Call for schedule and ticket prices.*

Hershey Theatre
15 East Caracas Avenue, Hershey, PA 17033. Tel: 717-534-3405.

Yet another of Hershey's extravagant architectural statements, this 1,900-seat theater presents Broadway touring shows, classical music, jazz and dance. *Sep–Apr. Call for schedule and ticket prices.*

Milton Hershey School
Founders Hall, Homestead Lane, Hershey, PA 17033.
Tel: 717-520-2000.

The story of Hershey's tuition-free school is told in a series of exhibits and a 30-minute film presented under the huge, unsupported dome of Founders Hall. *Jan–Mar daily 10am–3pm, Apr–Dec daily 9am–4pm. Free admission.*

ZooAmerica North American Wildlife Park
Park Avenue (Route 743), Hershey, PA 17033. Tel: 717-534-3860.

More than 200 animals from all over North America – bear, bison and other large mammals – are kept in recreated habitats. *Daily 10am–5pm, extended summer hours. $5.25 adults, $4.25 seniors, $4 children (age 3–12); free with Hersheypark admission if visitors enter from within the amusement park.*

OUTDOOR RECREATION

Hershey Country Club
1000 East Derry Road, Hershey, PA 17033. Tel: 717-533-2360.

Hershey is known as the "golf capital of Pennsylvania" owing largely to these three nationally ranked 18-hole golf courses.

SPECIAL EVENTS

February
Chocolate-Lovers Weekend
Hotel Hershey, Hotel Road,
Hershey, PA 17033.
Tel: 800-533-3131.

A three-night, family-oriented
package designed for incurable
chocoholics, with special meals,
games, tours, culinary demonstrations and workshops.

October
Gardenfest
Hershey Gardens, Hotel Road,
Hershey, PA 17033.
Tel: 717-534-3493.

Talks and demonstrations cover
the history of the gardens, flower
arranging, garden design and
related crafts.

November–December
Christmas at Hershey
Hersheypark, 100 West
Hersheypark Drive, Hershey, PA
17033. Tel: 717-534-3090.

The park is decorated with more
than a half-million Christmas
lights for this month-long extravaganza, with choral concerts,
puppet shows, ice-sculpting,
magic shows, live reindeer and,
of course, visits from Santa
Claus.

INFORMATION

Hershey Information Center
300 Park Boulevard, Hershey, PA
17033. Tel: 800-437-7439.

HIGHLIGHTS

- Gettysburg National Park
- Pennsylvania State Capitol
- City Island
- Winterthur
- Longwood Gardens
- Brandywine River Museum

Farther Afield

*P*ennsylvania Dutch Country is a convenient base for exploring several other getaway destinations. About 60 miles west of Lancaster, for example, is **Gettysburg**, Pennsylvania, site of one of the most significant battles of the American Civil War.

Make your first stop **Gettysburg National Military Park**, commemorating the spot where 70,000 Confederate troops led by Gen. Robert E. Lee encountered Gen. George G. Meade's 93,000 Union soldiers in July 1863. Tours trace the progress of the three-day battle, which expended 51,000 lives in the bloodiest engagement of the war. Several nearby attractions help interpret the battle, including **General Lee's Headquarters**, an 18th-century stone house that features an impressive collection of Civil War memorabilia; the **Jennie Wade House and Olde Town Square**, where you'll learn how a stray bullet accounted for the only civilian death of the battle; the **Lincoln Room Museum**, where the President completed his famous Gettysburg Address; and the **National Civil War Wax Museum**.

Don't miss an opportunity to stroll the charming old streets of Gettysburg, where you'll find shops packed with antiques,

Holiday decorations at Winterthur. Right, Helen, a 400-pound bronze pig, sits outside the Brandywine River Museum in Chadds Ford, Pennsylvania.

military memorabilia and historical art. A free walking tour of the historic district highlights more than 100 restored buildings. Nighttime candlelight tours are offered, too.

To see more of the surrounding countryside, take the self-guided 36-mile **Scenic Valley Tour**, or a 16- or 50-mile ride on the vintage **Gettysburg Railway**. If you travel in fall, you're sure to detect the sweet smell of apples, Adams County's No. 1 product, celebrated each October at the **Apple Harvest Festival** in Arendtsville.

Lincoln isn't the only President associated with Gettysburg. Dwight D. Eisenhower chose the area as his retirement home. In fact, his farm on the outskirts of town – now **Eisenhower National Historic Site** – is the only home he and his wife, Mamie, ever owned. A shuttle from the National Park Visitor Center takes visitors to the Georgian-style farmhouse, where the Eisenhowers entertained dignitaries such as Nikita Khrushchev, Charles DeGaulle, Winston Churchill and others.

The Eisenhower house reflects Ike's and Mamie's surprisingly simple tastes.

The elegant living room, a showcase for the couple's many priceless gifts from foreign heads of state, is said to have been the President's least favorite. The remainder of the home reflects Ike's and Mamie's surprisingly simple tastes.

Another nearby destination is Pennsylvania's capital, **Harrisburg**, about an hour's drive northwest of Lancaster via Route 283. In addition to fine restaurants, galleries, nightclubs and a fascinating variety of architecture, you'll find the **State Capitol, State Museum** and **Governor's Mansion**. Tours of all three are available.

Walk across the restored Walnut Street Bridge or take a bus, trolley or horse-drawn carriage to the city's riverfront gem, **City Island**. You can easily spend a day here taking in views of the Susquehanna River and Harrisburg skyline, or enjoying an impromptu lunch and live music around the rustic concession stands at

Inside the marble-clad rotunda of the Pennsylvania Capitol in Harrisburg.

RiverSide Village. Here too is the *Pride of the Susquehanna*, a 70-foot riverboat that offers a 45-minute river cruise. Water taxis and a 36-foot pontoon boat are also available. Or rent a kayak, canoe or sailboat at the north end of the island.

Other attractions include **RiverSide Stadium**, home of the Harrisburg Senators, a minor-league baseball team; and the **City**

Island Railroad, a diminutive, steam-driven train that travels on an oval track. It departs from the Railroad Depot just off the Walnut Street Bridge, where you'll also find the antique **Mengels Carousel**.

To the east of Lancaster County is the historic **Brandywine Valley**, which runs across the Pennsylvania border into Delaware. For such a compact area, it's packed with attractions. Highlights include **Winterthur**, a nine-story mansion transformed into a museum of decorative arts by Henry Francis duPont, who amassed a peerless collection of antiques made or used in America from 1640 to 1860. Among the treasures you'll find in some 200 period rooms and galleries are a set of silver tankards fashioned by Paul Revere and a 66-piece dinner service made for George Washington. The mansion is surrounded by more than 900 magnificent acres of woodland and gardens designed by duPont himself.

You'll find an even grander display of horticultural prowess at **Longwood Gardens**, yet another property owned and developed by a member of the duPont family, this time Pierre. More than 11,000 types of plants are displayed on 1,050 acres of breathtaking outdoor gardens, conservatories and illuminated fountains. Special happenings include a variety of holiday displays, elaborate summer fountain shows and a full schedule of music, dance and drama presented in an open-air venue modeled after an ancient Roman theater.

Union and Confederate "soldiers" clash during Civil War Heritage Days in Gettysburg.

Just a few miles from Longwood, in Chadds Ford, is the
Brandywine River Museum, housed in a Civil War-era gristmill
beautifully converted into gallery space with hand-hewn beams,
wide-plank floors and large glass panels with expansive views of
the river and rolling countryside. Much of the collection is dedicated to the Wyeth family, including illustrator and painter N.C.
and his son Andrew, best known for *Christina's World*. Other artists
associated with the region and shown here include Horace Pippin,
Frank Schoonover and Maxfield Parrish.

Just east of Chadds Ford is **Brandywine Battlefield State
Park**, site of an engagement between Continental and British
troops on September 11, 1777. Although Washington's force was
defeated, the battle prevented
the British from reaching vital
supplies of food, weapons and
equipment in Pennsylvania.
Displays at the visitor center and

**Although the Continental Army
was defeated at Brandywine,
the battle saved vital supplies
of food and equipment.**

at two restored buildings used as quarters by Washington and the
Marquis de Lafayette interpret life during the Revolution.

Other attractions in the Brandywine area include the **Hagley
Museum**, a restored 19th-century village where Eleuthère Irénée
Du Pont de Nemours established his first black-powder mill;
Nemours Mansion and Gardens, a 102-room château on 300 landscaped acres built by Alfred I. Du Pont in 1910; the **Mushroom
Museum at Phillips Place**, a museum and shop dedicated to the
history and cultivation of mushrooms and other gourmet items;
and the **Delaware Museum of Natural History**, with one of the
largest shell collections in the United States and exhibits on plants
and animals as far afield as the African savanna and the Great
Barrier Reef as well as the Delaware Valley.

Where to Stay

Farnsworth House Inn

401 Baltimore Street, Gettysburg, PA 17325. Tel: 717-334-8838.

The south wall of this brick house was riddled with more than 100 bullet holes during the Battle of Gettysburg when Confederate sharpshooters positioned in the attic fired on Union troops. Today, the house serves as an inn and restaurant. Decor in the nine guest rooms reflects the style of the Civil War period – wood floors, canopy beds, Victorian antiques and memorabilia. An airy sun room is filled with greenery and wicker furnishings. A full country breakfast is served in the dining room or, weather permitting, in a lovely garden. The restaurant specializes in early-American cuisine served by waiters in period costume. Tours of the garret – now a museum – are offered daily, and guests are often treated to an evening of ghost stories. *Rates: $85 double occupancy. Children are welcome with advance notice; no pets. Amenities: nine rooms with private bath and air conditioning. Restaurant, garden, deck, parking. AE, Dis, MC, V.*

Harrisburg Hilton and Towers

One North Second Street, Harrisburg, PA 17101.
Tel: 717-233-6000 or toll-free 800-445-8667. Fax: 717-233-6271.

A spiffy modern hotel in downtown Harrisburg designed for executive travelers but popular with families, too. The largest and most luxurious rooms are in the uppermost floors or Towers, which have spacious sitting areas, contemporary furnishings, an exclusive lounge and free continental breakfast. Fine dining is available at the Golden Sheaf. Families may prefer the more casual Market Square Cafe or Raspberries. *Rates: $139–$205 double occupancy. No charge for children 18 and under in the same room as parents or grandparents. Amenities: 341 rooms and suites with private bath, air conditioning, minibar and cable television. Indoor pool, fitness room, three restaurants and piano bar, extensive conference facilities, parking. All major credit cards.*

⭐ Sweetwater Farm

Sweetwater Road, Glen Mills, PA 19342. Tel: 610-459-4711 or toll-free 800-793-3892. Fax: 610-358-4945.

Fifty acres of pasture and cropland sprawl around this extraordinary stone mansion, originally built in 1734, with an addition in 1815. Guests have a choice of three settings. Rooms in the 1734 wing have a snug colonial feeling, with random-width wood floors, four-poster beds, quilts and period reproductions. The 1815 wing reflects the grander and more dignified style of the Georgian period. Rooms here have 12-foot ceilings, fireplaces, polished wood floors and four-poster beds. Four cottages range in size and style from the spacious two-bedroom "Greenhouse" with living room, kitchen and fireplace to the cozy but appealing "Herb," which has a double bed and sitting area. Guests are invited to lounge in front of the fire in one of two parlors or the handsome library. A breakfast of eggs, waffles, sausage and muffins is served in a formal dining room or by a brick hearth in the kitchen. *Rates: $180–$275 double occupancy (ask about midweek discount). Children are welcome; pets in the cottages only. Amenities: 11 rooms or cottages with private bath, air conditioning and television, some with fireplace; three cottages with kitchen. Pool, garden, patio, parking. AE, MC, V.*

Where to Eat

☆ **Chadds Ford Inn**
Routes 1 and 100, Chadds Ford, PA 19317. Tel: 610-388-7361.

The paintings of the Wyeth family grace the walls of this old stone tavern, built in the early 1700s and raided by British troops during the Battle of Brandywine. Windsor chairs, recessed windows and low ceilings create a snug colonial feeling in the dining rooms and back tavern. The menu isn't extensive but is well-prepared, combining traditional and contemporary flavors in such dishes as stuffed quail with cornbread and andouille, pork chops with mustard-maple demiglaze, fried-leek ravioli, and pan-roasted catfish with orange-pecan sauce. Save room for dessert, freshly prepared by in-house pastry chefs. *Moderate–expensive. Lunch Mon–Fri 11:30am–2pm, Sat 11:30am–2:30pm, Sun brunch 11am–2pm; dinner Mon–Thu 5:30pm–10pm, Fri–Sat 5pm–10:30pm, Sun 4pm–9pm. Bar and wine list. Reservations recommended. All major credit cards.*

☆ **Dilworthtown Inn**
1390 Old Wilmington Pike, West Chester, PA 19382. Tel: 610-399-1390.

Fine Continental cuisine and a wine cellar with more than 800 labels are the big attractions at this restored 18th-century tavern just a short drive from Longwood Gardens and the Brandywine Battlefield. The 15 candlelit dining rooms, all furnished in elegant early-American style, some with fireplaces, set the stage for such beautifully presented favorites as crab cakes with caramelized tomato and mango chutney, grilled veal chop with herbed polenta, or swordfish with a macadamia-and-parmesan crust in lemon-caper sauce. Don't overlook appetizers – the shrimp bisque and crisp lobster with toasted sesame sauce are particularly enticing. There's a worthy list of nightly specials, too. A fine choice for romantic dining. *Expensive. Mon–Fri 5:30pm–9:30pm, Sat 5pm–9:30pm, Sun 3pm–9pm. Bar and extensive wine list. Reservations recommended. All major credit cards.*

Dobbin House Tavern
89 Steinwehr Avenue, Gettysburg, PA 17325. Tel: 717-334-2100

Built in 1776 and listed on the National Register of Historic Places, this venerable stone house is now divided into two main sections. Upstairs you'll find fine dining in a homey

☆ indicates a personal favorite of the author

colonial setting, often warmed by a crackling fire in a few of the seven fireplaces. The menu gravitates toward hearty American fare: roast duck with apple-cider sauce, Maryland crab cakes, filet mignon, broiled lamb chops. The atmosphere is more casual downstairs in the Spring House Tavern, which features lighter and less expensive choices like barbecued ribs, spit-roasted chicken, and a variety of hefty sandwiches and salads. Feeling adventurous? Try the Philadelphia fish house punch – a potent combination of rum, brandy and fruit juices. *Moderate. Tavern daily 11:30am–10pm; dining room daily 5pm–9pm. Bar and wine list. Reservations recommended. AE, MC, V.*

pol–i–tesse

540 Race Street, Harrisburg, PA 17109. Tel: 717-236-2048.

Situated in Shipoke on the outskirts of downtown Harrisburg, this intimate 14-table restaurant serves innovative American cuisine with a few ethnic twists. An extensive wine list harmonizes well with the eclectic choice of entrees, featuring dishes like pan-seared trout, cheesy crab and lobster atop a portobello mushroom cap, veal chop with apple-cider demiglaze, and grilled eggplant layered with Chevre and wild mushroom polenta. The mood is sophisticated but casual, with linen tablecloths and bright, contemporary art. Clientele include suit-clad legislators as well as local folks in jeans. Outdoor seating accommodates overflow crowds in warmer months. *Moderate–expensive. Lunch Tue–Fri 11:30am–2pm; dinner Tue–Sat 5pm–9pm.*

Extensive wine list. Reservations recommended. All major credit cards.

Pub and Restaurant

20-22 Lincoln Square, Gettysburg, PA 17325. Tel: 717-334-7100.

An aged, well-trod place, the menu at this historic inn on Lincoln Square is an elaboration on pub grub – Buffalo wings, burgers, sandwiches, salads and a few Mexican choices. Dinner entrees like chicken Marsala, shrimp scampi and fettuccine Alfredo are a bit more ambitious though not particularly inspired. Dessert presents slightly more interesting possibilities, like New York cheesecake, Kentucky Derby pie, chocolate-peanut-butter layer cake. *Budget–moderate. Mon–Sat 11am–midnight (bar until 2am), Sun noon–10pm. Bar and wine list. Reservations for six or more only. AE, MC, V.*

Scott's Bar & Grille

212 Locust Street, Harrisburg, PA 17101. Tel: 717-234-7599.

Urban professionals flock to this smart bar and restaurant in downtown Harrisburg. Pick at munchies or pick up new friends over hot and cold finger foods during the weekday happy hour. Conversation fills the bar and spills out onto the shady deck. For less talk and more food, repair to the relative calm of the dining room, where attentive waiters serve salads, sandwiches, burgers and other light fare, as well as an eclectic mix of entrees, including grilled salmon Hollandaise, stir-fried cashew chicken, seafood fettuccine and blackened catfish with butter pecan sauce. Dessert is nicely paired with a frothy cappuccino.

Moderate. Lunch Mon–Fri 11:30am–3pm; dinner Mon–Thu 5pm–10pm, Fri–Sat 5pm–11pm. Bar open to 2am. Reservations recommended. All major credit cards.

What to Do

ATTRACTIONS

Brandywine Battlefield State Park
Route 1, P.O. Box 202, Chadds Ford, PA 19317. Tel: 610-459-3342.

Continental and British troops clashed here in September 1777. Historic structures include the headquarters of George Washington and the Marquis de Lafayette, both with exhibits on life during the late 18th century. *Tue–Sat 9am–5pm, Sun noon–5pm. Guided tours $3.50 adults, $1.50 children (age 6–12).*

Brandywine River Museum
Routes 1 and 100, P.O. Box 141, Chadds Ford, PA 19317.
Tel: 610-388-2700.

N.C. Wyeth, Andrew Wyeth, Horace Pippin and Maxfield Parrish are just a few of the dozens of regional artists whose work is exhibited at this restored 19th-century gristmill. *Daily 9:30am–4:30pm. $5 adults, $2.50 seniors and students.*

City Island

A 63-acre island on the Susquehanna River, with marinas, riverboat cruises, hiking and biking trails, horse-and-buggy rides, a minor-league baseball stadium, miniature railroad, antique carousel and other family-oriented facilities. For information, call the Harrisburg Parks and Recreation Department, tel: 717-255-3020.

Eisenhower National Historic Site
Route 15, Gettysburg, PA 17325.
Tel: 717-338-9114.

Dwight and Mamie Eisenhower retired to this 500-acre farm outside Gettysburg in 1961. Visitors must buy tickets and take a shuttle bus from the visitor center at Gettysburg National Military Park. *Feb–Dec, call for exact schedule. $5.25 adults, $3.25 children (age 13–16) $2.25 children (age 6–12).*

General Lee's Headquarters
401 Buford Avenue, Gettysburg, PA 17325. Tel: 717-334-3141.

Firearms, sabers, uniforms and other Civil War artifacts are displayed at this 18th-century stone house, occupied by Robert E. Lee during the Battle of Gettysburg. The second floor is now open for overnight lodging. *Mar–Nov daily 9am–9pm. $3 adults, 50¢ children under 12.*

Gettysburg National Military Park
95 Taneytown Road, Gettysburg, PA 17325. Tel: 717-334-1124.

The 3,500-acre park commemorates the July 1863 battle between Confederate and Union armies, the bloodiest of the American Civil War. Stop first at the visitor center for information about ranger-guided talks and walks or a self-guided tour of the battle-field and Gettysburg National Cemetery, where Abraham Lincoln delivered his famous speech. *Visitor center daily 8am–5pm, battlefield 6am–10pm.*

Gettysburg Railway
106 North Washington Street, Gettysburg, PA 17325.
Tel: 717-334-6932.

This vintage steam-powered railroad runs between Gettys-burg and Biglerville, a 16-mile round-trip. *Apr–Oct; call for ticket prices and exact schedule. Inquire about dinner, holiday and various theme trains as well as a special four-hour trip to Peach Glen.*

Hagley Museum
Route 141, P.O. Box 3630, Wilmington, DE 19807.
Tel: 302-658-2400.

A 19th-century village developed around the gunpowder mills of French emigrant Eleuthère Irénée Du Pont de Nemours, founder of the Du Ponts' American empire. The 230-acre site includes recreations and restorations of original build-ings and machinery as well as Du Pont's elegant Georgian mansion, **Eleutherian Mills**, built in 1803 and furnished in several period styles. *Mid-Mar–Dec daily 9:30am– 4:30pm, Jan–mid-Mar Mon–Fri 1pm–4pm, Sat–Sun 9:30am– 4:30pm. $9.75 adults, $7.50 students and seniors, $3.50 children (age 6–14).*

Jennie Wade House and Olde Town Square
Baltimore Street, Gettysburg, PA 17325. Tel: 717-334-4100.

Virginia Wade, the only civilian casualty of Gettysburg, was killed by a stray bullet in the kitchen of this little house, now fully restored in period style. The site also features a recreation of several 19th-century village shops, including a barber, printer and country store. *Mar–Nov daily 9am–5pm, extended summer hours. Call for admission fee.*

Lincoln Room Museum
12 Lincoln Square, Gettysburg, PA 17325. Tel: 717-334-8188.

Abraham Lincoln completed the Gettysburg Address at this site, restored with many original furnishings. *Mon–Fri 9am–4pm; extended summer hours. $3.25 adults, $3 seniors, $2 students, $1.75 children (age 7–11).*

Longwood Gardens
Route 1, P.O. Box 501, Kennett Square, PA 19348.
Tel: 610-388-1000.

A 1,050-acre property with gorgeous outdoor gardens, four acres of conservatories, elaborate fountains, historic structures and a children's garden. Inquire about fountain shows, holiday displays and performances at the 2,100-seat classical amphitheater. *Outdoor gardens daily 9am–5pm, conservatories 10am–5pm (to 6pm Apr–Oct). Both may be open later for special events and holiday displays. $12 adults ($8 on Tue), $6 youths (age 16–20), $2 children (age 6–15).*

Mushroom Museum at Phillips Place
909 East Baltimore Pike (Route 1), Kennett Square, PA 19348.
Tel: 610-388-6082.

Exhibits and shop dedicated to the history and cultivation of mushrooms and other gourmet items. *Daily 10am–6pm. $1.25*

Classic Pennsylvania barn in Middletown, south of Harrisburg.

adults, 75¢ seniors, 50¢ children (age 7–12).

National Civil War Wax Museum
297 Steinwehr Avenue, Gettysburg, PA 17325. Tel: 717-334-6245.
Some 30 wax-figure dioramas recount the history of the war. *Mar–Dec daily 9am–5pm, extended summer hours; Jan–Feb Sat–Sun 9am–5pm. $4.50 adults, $3.50 seniors, $2.50 students (age 13–17), $1.75 children (age 6–12).*

Nemours Mansion and Gardens
Rockland Road, P.O. Box 109, Wilmington, DE 19899.
Tel: 302-651-6912.
Alfred I. Du Pont built this extravagant Louis XVI-style château in 1910. Like other Du Pont properties, it is graced with an extraordinary collection of art and antiques and, in this case, a splendid French garden. Guided tours are available. *May–Nov Tue–Sun, tours at 9am, 11am, 1pm and 3pm (no 9am tour on Sun). $10 per person. Visitors must be age 16 or older.*

Pride of the Susquehanna
Harrisburg Area Riverboat Society, P.O. Box 910, Harrisburg, PA 17108. Tel: 717-234-6500.
This 77-foot paddlewheeler takes passengers on a 45-minute narrated cruise on the Susquehanna River. Tickets are available at the dock on City Island. *Jun–Aug, Tue–Sun, departures at noon, 1pm, 3pm. Call for schedule*

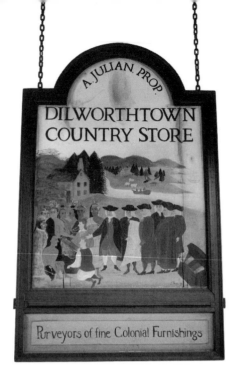

State Museum of Pennsylvania
Third and North Streets,
Harrisburg, PA 17108.
Tel: 717-787-4980.

Exhibits on a variety of topics – archaeology, science, natural history and more – are drawn from the state's permanent collection as well as traveling shows. Inquire about planetarium shows. *Tue–Sat 9am–5pm, Sun noon–5pm. Free admission.*

Winterthur Museum
Route 52, Winterthur, DE 19735.
Tel: 302-888-4600 or toll-free
800-448-3883.

One of the world's best collections of American antiques is displayed at this nine-story mansion, the former country estate of Henry Francis Du Pont. Much of the collection is displayed in dozens of period rooms, seen by guided tour only. Visitors can wander freely about the galleries. The first floor gives an overview of American decorative arts; the second focuses on distinct styles and traditions. You may need another day to explore the gardens – some 900 acres designed by Du Pont in a naturalistic English style. *Mon–Sat 9am–5pm, Sun noon–5pm. $13 adults, $11 students, $9 children (age 5–11).*

in May, Sep and Oct, and for dinner cruise reservations. $4.95 adults, $3 children (age 2–12).

RiverSide Stadium
City Island, P.O. Box 15757,
Harrisburg, PA 17105.
Tel: 717-231-4444.

Fed up with the majors? Check out the double-A Harrisburg Senators at this ballpark on City Island. *Apr–Sep. $3–$8.*

State Capitol
Third and State Streets, Harrisburg,
PA 17101. Tel: 717-787-6810.

Built in 1906, the Pennsylvania capitol is a grand domed structure modeled loosely on St. Peter's Basilica in Rome. The tour covers the rotunda and both houses of the legislature. *Tours every 30 minutes Mon–Fri 8:30am–4pm, Sat–Sun hourly 9am–4pm (except noon). Free admission.*

SPECIAL EVENTS

May
Gettysburg Outdoor Antique Show
Gettysburg Travel Council.
Tel: 717-334-6274.

More than 175 dealers of antiques and collectibles gather on the streets of downtown Gettysburg.

Winterthur Point-to-Point Race
Winterthur Museum, Winterthur, DE. Tel: 800-448-3883.

The main event is amateur steeplechase racing, but there are also pony races, a parade of antique carriages, and special tours of the gardens and galleries.

June–July
Civil War Heritage Days
Gettysburg Travel Council. Tel: 717-334-6274.

A weeklong celebration with a living–history encampment, battle reenactment, memorabilia and book shows, lectures by prominent historians, concerts, fireworks and other events.

Country Pride Pops
Winterthur Museum, Winterthur, DE. Tel: 800-448-3883.

A day of popular symphonic music, with an outdoor crafts festival.

September
Reenactment of the Battle of Brandywine
Brandywine Battlefield State Park, Chadds Ford, PA. Tel: 610-459-3342.

About 400 "soldiers" reenact the battle at this daylong event. Other activities include musket drills, artillery demonstrations, historical plays, a recreated Quaker meeting, craft shows and more.

September–October
GardenFest
Longwood Gardens, Kennett Square, PA. Tel: 610-388-1000.

Experts give daily talks and demonstrations on gardening. Weekends feature live music and displays of seasonal fruits and flowers.

October
Apple Harvest Festival
South Mountain Fairgrounds, Route 234, Arendtsville, PA. Call the Gettysburg Travel Council, tel: 717-334-6274.

An old-time country fair with craft shows, scarecrow making, tractor pulls, live entertainment, pie-eating contests and just about every kind of food made with apples.

October–November
Chrysanthemum Festival
Longwood Gardens, Kennett Square, PA. Tel: 610-388-1000.

An autumn celebration with displays of more than 15,000 chrysanthemums, special performances, demonstrations and children's activities.

INFORMATION

Brandywine Valley Tourist Information Center
Longwood and Greenwood Roads, P.O. Box 910, Kennett Square, PA 19348. Tel: 610-388-2900.

Gettysburg Travel Council
35 Carlisle Street, Gettysburg, PA 17325. Tel: 717-334-6274.

Harrisburg-Hershey-Carlisle Convention and Tourism Bureau
114 Walnut Street, Harrisburg, PA 17108. Tel: 717-975-8161.

Ten Great Getaways

1. Shop 'Til You Drop

You can easily spend a weekend trawling the little shops in Bird-in-Hand, Intercourse and other small towns, but serious bargain-hunters may want to concentrate their efforts at one or more of the area's many outlet centers – Rockvale Square Outlets and Tanger Outlet Center on Route 30 in Lancaster, and Vanity Fair Outlet Village, Reading Outlet Center and Manufacturers Outlet Mall in and around Reading – or at the raucous Green Dragon Market in Ephrata and Root's Country Market in Manheim.

2. About the Amish

Want to learn more about the Amish and Mennonites? The following places offer accurate information about the life and culture of Lancaster's Plain People:

The People's Place
3513 Old Philadelphia Pike, Intercourse, PA. Tel: 717-768-7171.

An interactive museum and a documentary film, *Who Are the Amish?*, interpret the culture of the Plain People and explore differences among various Amish and Mennonite groups. There's a fine bookstore and craft shop, too.

Mennonite Information Center
2209 Millstream Road, Lancaster, PA. Tel: 717-299-0954.

Owned and operated by Plain folks, the center can arrange a Mennonite guide to ride in your car for a two-hour tour of Pennsylvania Dutch Country.

Amish Farm and House
2395 Route 30 East, Lancaster, PA 17602. Tel: 717-394-6185.

One of the better attractions that claim to represent "genuine" Amish culture, this place offers tours of an Amish house and working farm.

Amish Country Tours
Route 340 at Plain and Fancy Farm, Lancaster, PA. Tel: 717-768-3600.

Daily two-hour tours along the back roads of Amish Country.

An 18th-century gristmill at Mill Bridge Village, a popular tourist attraction outside Strasburg.

3. Wine-Tasting Tour

Oenophiles can make the rounds of several wineries in the area; all offer free tours and tastings.

Nissley Winery
140 Vintage Drive, Bainbridge, PA 17502. Tel: 717-426-3514.

Mount Hope Estate and Winery
Route 72, Manheim, PA.
Tel: 717-665-7021.

Twin Brook Winery
5697 Strasburg Road, RD 2, Box 2376, Gap, PA. Tel: 717-442-4915.

Lancaster County Winery
Rawlinsville Road, Willow Street, PA. Tel: 717-464-3555.

Pinnacle Ridge Winery
407 Old Route 22, Kutztown, PA.
Tel: 717-756-4481.

Clover Hill Vineyards and Winery
RD 1, Box 299, West Meadow Road, Robesonia, PA.
Tel: 610-693-8382.

4. "To Market, To Market . . ."

You'll find the area's best produce at several farmers' markets. Some also feature handmade quilts, furniture and other crafts as well as clothing, antiques and a host of other merchandise. Here are a few of the best:

Bird-in-Hand Farmers' Market
Maple Avenue (Route 340), Bird-in-Hand, PA. Tel: 717-393-9674.

A rather tame experience catering to tourists rather than local folks. *Fri–Sat year-round, Wed Apr–Nov, Thu Jul–Oct 8:30am–5:30pm.*

Central Market
William Henry Place, Lancaster, PA. Tel: 717-291-4723.

Listed in the National Register of Historic Places, the oldest continuously operating farmers' market in the country is located in the heart of the city of Lancaster. *Tue and Fri 6am–4pm, Sat 6am–2pm.*

Farmers' Market at Doneckers
100 N. State Street, Ephrata, PA 17522. Tel: 717-738-9555.

Piles of fresh produce, meats, seafood and baked goods at the Artworks complex. *Thu 8am–6pm, Fri 8am–8pm, Sat 8am–5pm.*

Green Dragon Market and Auction
955 N. State Street, Ephrata, PA.
Tel: 717-738-1117.

A boisterous, sprawling market with everything from fresh meats, produce and baked goods to auctions of farm animals and equipment. A fascinating experience. *Fri 10am–10pm.*

Meadow Brook Farmers' Market
345 W. Main Street, Leola, PA.
Tel: 717-656-2226.

A classic, small-town market with piles of fresh produce. *Fri 8am–6pm, Sat 8am–5pm.*

Root's Country Market & Auction
705 Graystone Road, Manheim, PA. Tel: 717-898-7811.

Vendors of all types make this a lively affair, with lots of home-grown produce, crafts and second-hand stuff. *Tue 9am–9pm.*

5. Kid Stuff

Pennsylvania Dutch Country is very child-friendly. Although some bed-and-breakfasts discourage guests from bringing young kids, there's usually no problem finding good, affordable lodging and dining. The most popular family destination is undoubtedly **Hershey**, which features a state-of-the-art amusement park, a high-tech ride through the chocolate-making process, a zoo and, of course, loads of candy. There are several lesser-known places, too. Kids will get a kick out of the interactive exhibits at the **Hands-on House** (717-569-5437) and will be intrigued by the planetarium, children's discovery room and other science-related exhibits at the **North Museum** at Franklin and Marshall College (717-291-3941), both in Lancaster. Buggy rides are usually a sure-fire hit with children; try **Abe's Buggy Rides** (717-392-1794), **Aaron & Jessica's Buggy Rides** (717-768-8828), or **Ed's Buggy Rides** (717-687-0360). Also popular is a ride on the vintage **Strasburg Railroad** (717-687-7522) or a visit to the nearby **Railroad Museum of Pennsylvania** (717-687-8628) and **National Toy Train Museum** (717-687-8976). Two places in Lititz are worth finding: Kids can satisfy their sweet tooth at the **Wilbur Chocolate Company** (717-626-3249) or try their hand at pretzel-twisting at the **Sturgis Pretzel House** (717-626-4354). And finally, there is **Dutch Wonderland** (717-291-1888) on Route 30, an old-fashioned amusement park with some 25 rides and water slides, a high-diving show and elaborate gardens.

6. Antiquers' Delight

You'll find antique shops just about everywhere in Pennsylvania Dutch Country, but the greatest concentration is in the northeastern corner of Lancaster County from Brickerville to Ephrata along Route 322 and from Ephrata to Adamstown along Route 272. Thousands of dealers swarm the "Adamstown Antique Mile" each week along Route 272 between Denver and Ephrata. Some of the larger dealers include Muddy Creek Antiques, Antique Showcase at the Black Horse, Weaver's Antique Mall and Stoudtburg Antiques Mall and Village.

7. Covered Bridge Tour

Lancaster has more covered bridges than any other county in Pennsylvania. Most were built in the 19th century and employ the Burr truss design. You may not get to all 28 during your visit, but here are some of the most scenic:

Baumgardner's Mill
Covered Bridge Road, east of Marticville.

Colemanville
Fox Hollow Road, south of Colemanville.

Eberly's Cider Mill
Cider Mill Road, south of Murrell.

Erb's
Erb's Bridge Road, north of Rothsville.

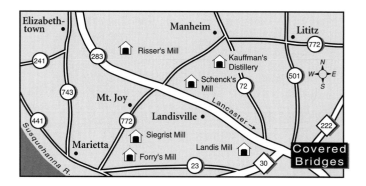

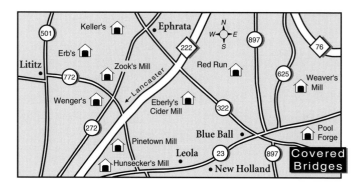

Forry's Mill
Bridge Valley Road, west of
Silver Spring.

Herr's Mill
Old South Ronks Road, south of
Soudersburg.

Hunsecker's Mill
Hunsecker Road, northeast of
Eden.

Jackson's Sawmill
Mount Pleasant Road, east of
Quarryville.

Kauffman's Distillery
Sun Hill Road, southwest of
Manheim.

Keller's
Rettew Mill Road, north of Akron.

Kurtz's Mill
Kiwanis Drive, Lancaster County
Central Park, just south of
Lancaster.

Lime Valley
Brenaman Road, Lime Valley.

Mercer's Fording
Creek Road, south of Christiana.

Neff's Mill
Penn Grant Road, southeast of
Lampeter.

Paradise
Belmont Road, northeast of
Paradise.

Pine Grove
Asheville Road, Pine Grove.

Pinetown Mill
Creek Road, south of Oregon.

Pool Forge
Pool Forge Road, west of
Churchtown.

Red Run
Red Run Road, north of Martindale.

Rose Hill
Log Cabin Road, west of
Brownstone.

Shenck's Mill
Erisman Road, north of Salunga.

Siegrist Mill
Siegrist Road, northwest of
Silver Spring.

Weaver's Mill
Weaverland Road, north of
Goodville.

Willows
Route 30, 1/2 mile west of the
896/Route 30 intersection.

White Rock
White Rock Road, southwest of
Union.

Zook's Mill
Lincoln Road, north of Rothsville.

8. Fall Frolic

Autumn is a great time to visit
Pennsylvania Dutch Country.
Tourist traffic slows, and the
foliage is spectacular. You'll find
gorgeous views at several overlooks along the Susquehanna
River, including **Pinnacle**

Overlook and **Susquehannock
State Park** in southern Lancaster
and **Chickies Rock County Park**
just north of Columbia, or up
on **Hawk Mountain** in Berks
County during the fall migration of eagles, falcons and other
birds of prey.

This is also the time when many
rural towns hold annual harvest
festivals, with everything from
amusement-park rides, parades
and live music to livestock and
produce competitions. It's a
real slice of Americana. Some of
the most popular events are
the **Elizabethtown Community
Fair, Denver Fair, Solanco**
(Southern Lancaster County)
Fair, Ephrata Fair (Pennsylvania's largest street fair), **West
Lampeter Fair, New Holland
Farmers Fair,** and **Manheim
Community Farm Show.**

Some farmers also offer hayrides
and other special events in fall.
One of the biggest attractions
is the **Pumpkin Train** – a special
ride aboard the Strasburg
Railroad to Cherry Crest Farm
(717-687-6843), where visitors
can wander through a cornfield
maze, pick pumpkins and take
hayrides.

9. Romantic Hideaway

Trying to rekindle an old flame
or spark up a new one? Try
pampering yourselves at one of
the area's many bed-and-
breakfast inns. The **Inn at Twin
Linden** in Churchtown is a
particularly good choice. Plush
rooms are furnished with a
stylish combination of tradition-

Amish boys gather at the spring sale in Gordonville.

al and contemporary styles. Jacuzzis and fireplaces are available in some rooms; ask for the Palladian Suite for an extra measure of elegance. Breakfast is a gourmet delight; many dishes are drawn from the innkeeper's cookbook. Intimate, candlelight dining is offered on Saturday night.

Another fine choice is the **Cameron Estate Inn**, a glorious 17-room inn listed on the National Register of Historic Places and furnished in lavish 19th-century style; the Mary Cameron Room is particularly lovely. Elegant dining is offered fireside in the first-floor restaurant.

10. Historic Highlights

History is everywhere in Pennsylvania Dutch Country, from 200-year-old farmhouses and ancient mills to excellent museums. It's easy to spend a week or so visiting historic sites, but if time is limited, try not to miss these highlights:

Hans Herr House

1849 Hans Herr Drive, Willow Street, PA 17584. Tel: 717-464-4438.

The earliest European settlement in Lancaster County, established in the early 18th century by Mennonite Bishop Hans Herr.

Landis Valley Museum

2451 Kissel Hill Road, Lancaster, PA 17601. Tel: 717-569-0401.

Life in a rural 19th-century village is brought to life with tools and equipment, many original buildings and demonstrations of blacksmithing, weaving, wool spinning and other crafts.

Historic Lancaster Walking Tour

Information Center, Southern Market House, 100 South Queen Street. Tel: 717-392-1776.

An informative 90-minute tour of downtown Lancaster's historic district.

Rock Ford Plantation

881 Rockford Road, Lancaster, PA 17608. Tel: 717-392-7223.

The gracious, Georgian-style home of Edward Hand, Irish-born doctor and George Washington's adjutant-general. The adjacent Kauffman Collection of fraktur, glassware, tin work, furniture and other 18th- and 19th-century crafts is housed in the barn.

Wheatland

1120 Marietta Avenue, Lancaster, PA 17603. Tel: 717-392-8721.

The home of James Buchanan, 15th President of the United States.

Lititz Museum

145 East Main Street, Lititz, PA 17543. Tel: 717-627-4636.

A fascinating collection of Lititz artifacts, with an emphasis on Moravian settlement. The Lititz Moravian Church, Linden Hall, Johannes Mueller House and other historic sites are within a few steps of the museum.

Ephrata Cloister

632 Main Street, Ephrata, PA 17522. Tel: 717-733-6600.

Home of an 18th-century monastic community known for music, printing, fraktur and an austere way of life.

Railroad Museum of Pennsylvania

Route 741, Box 15, Strasburg, PA 17579. Tel: 717-687-8628.

The state's finest collection of vintage rail cars and locomotives.

Index

About The Contributors

Margaret Gates spent five years at the *Daily News* in Lebanon, Pennsylvania, before taking a position as a feature writer at the *Lancaster New Era.*

Susan Jurgelski is a feature writer at the *Lancaster New Era.* Her work has been recognized by several organizations, including the National Federation of Press Women, Pennsylvania Newspaper Publishers Association and the Society of Professional Journalists.

John Gattuso has written or edited eight books, including travel guides to Philadelphia, New York City and the National Parks. He is the editor of Stone Creek Publications in Milford, New Jersey, and author of *Getaway Guides: New Hope and Bucks County.*

Few people can write with such authority about the Amish as **Donald Kraybill,** former director of the Young Center for the Study of Anabaptist and Pietist Groups and author of several books about the Amish, including *The Riddle of Amish Culture* and *The Puzzles of Amish Life.* He is currently provost of Messiah College in Grantham, Pennsylvania.

Keith Baum grew up in the heart of Amish country in the little village of Intercourse, Pennsylvania. He was a staff photographer at Lancaster Newspapers for 10 years, and his work appears regularly in calendars, magazines and other publications, including a new book, *Lancaster County.* Currently, Keith is a free-lance photographer and a member of SEND International's media team. A dozen of his photos are on permanent display at the National Museum of American History in Washington, D.C.

Mimi Brodeur writes about food and restaurants for the *Patriot-News* in Harrisburg, Pennsylvania. Her work has also appeared in *Food and Wine* and *Pittsburgh Magazine.*

Peggy Schmidt has been a staff writer and columnist at the *Sunday News* in Lancaster, Pennsylvania, for more than 20 years.

Judith Rollman is a reviewer and columnist for the *Reading Eagle-Times.*

A Lancaster County native, **Rochelle Shenk** has been an editor and writer for more than 15 years. She writes for several publications in central Pennsylvania, including a restaurant column for *Lancaster County Magazine.*

Mary Alice Bitts is an editor and columnist at *Lancaster County Magazine* and an arts correspondent for Lancaster Newspapers. She is a published poet and composer, a jewelry designer, and the public relations director of the Poetry Continuum, a nonprofit literary group.

Getaway Guides:
New Hope and Bucks County

GETAWAY GUIDES

New Hope and Bucks County

By John Gattuso ◆ Photographs by Wink Einthoven

"Don't leave home without it!"
The Beacon

"[Filled with] treasures on and off the beaten path."
Express-Times

"All the ins and outs, highs and lows . . . in a breezy, easy-to-read manner."
New Hope Gazette

Quantity	Title		Unit Price	Total
_____	New Hope and Bucks County		$12.95	_____
_____	Pennsylvania Dutch Country		$12.95	_____
			Subtotal	_____
			6% Sales Tax (NJ only)	_____
			TOTAL	_____

Name _____

Address _____

City/State/Zip _____

Telephone _____

Make checks payable to: Stone Creek Publications, 460 Shire Road, Milford, NJ 08848. Tel: 908-995-0016. E-mail: stocreek@aol.com.